Internal Audit of Treasury and cash management

BENTALHA BADR

Internal Audit of Treasury and cash management

All rights reserved. No reproduction, copy, or transmission of this publication may be made without written permission.
Internal Audit of Treasury and cash management
Contact: bentalhabadr@gmail.com
© Badr BENTALHA, 2022
ISBN: 9798363213779

Internal Audit of Treasury and cash management

BENTALHA BADR

Internal Audit of Treasury and cash management

DEDICATION

For my parents,
For my wife and my two daughters,
For my sister and my brother,
For my friends and colleagues.

CONTENTS

ACKNOWLEDGMENTS	viii
PREFACE	x
INTRODUCTION	1

Part One: The theoretical framework of the internal audit of the cash cycle — 7

Chapter 1: Theoretical and conceptual approaches to internal auditing	9
Chapter 2: The company's treasury	34
Chapter 3: Internal audit of the treasury cycle	42

Part two: Internal Audit of the Treasury Cycle, Practical Aspects — 60

Chapter 1: Methodology, objectives and detailed approach of the cash cycle audit	61
Chapter 2: A practical approach to the internal audit of the cash cycle	66
Chapter 3: Recommendations and perspectives of the internal audit of the treasury cycle	144
CONCLUSION	150
BIBLIOGRAPHIC REFERENCES	153
TABLE OF CONTENTS	158

ACKNOWLEDGMENTS

At the outset, it is appropriate to express thanks to several people. First, I would like to thank those who participated in my training and opened the way to scientific research. Special thanks are also addressed to my colleagues, researchers, and academics who try every day through their scientific writings to participate in the edification of scientific research in the world.

I also thank my parents, my wife, my two daughters, my family, my friends, and all the people who helped me overcome the difficulties and make this work succeed.

Finally, I would like to thank all those who spent time reviewing the various chapters, especially for their constructive comments and observations.

Internal Audit of Treasury and cash management

PREFACE

In the contemporary context, the treasurer has a great opportunity and a high level of responsibility. The treasurer's duties are many and varied, ranging from cash management to risk management. Internal auditing of the treasury cycle is primarily aimed at ensuring that treasury activities are operating efficiently and that predefined standards are being respected.

The author provides practitioners and students with the fundamental knowledge and insight into the skills required to conduct a successful internal audit of the treasury. This manual is primarily intended for students, practitioners, and managers to help clarify the process of internal auditing the treasury cycle.

The book is a synthesis of years of study and practical experience to allow the different actors to discover the internal audit of the treasury and to understand the mechanisms, objectives, and approaches of this operational audit.

The book is divided into two parts. In the first part, we discuss the different conceptual and theoretical notions of internal audit, treasury, and internal audit. In the second part, we present the empirical part of the internal audit of the treasury by proposing a global and integrated model of the internal audit of the treasury function.

INTRODUCTION

Internal auditing is a relatively recent function and activity. The beginning of academic discussions around this concept dates back to the Great Depression of the 1930s. The effects of this crisis severely damaged the financial health of companies and economies. The crisis also raised doubts about the steering and management mechanisms used. As a result, large companies started to call upon external auditing firms to certify accounts and reduce costs.

A great deal of attention was subsequently paid to auditing and auditors. The latter had the privilege to give some assurance to the markets and shareholders. Nevertheless, the scandals of the 2000s and especially the great economic and moral collapse of the Anderson firm in the United States have changed the dominant perception of auditing assignments. Indeed, doubts have arisen about the impartiality and rigor of auditors and the certifications conducted. In addition, the Enron, Tyco, and WorldCom scandals revealed the shortcomings of audit professionals and also led to a rethinking of the existing audit models at the time. The collapse of Lehman Brothers, the financial crash of 2008, and the Greek public accounts have renewed these doubts about the ability of auditing to detect and correct the shortcomings observed. The magnitude of these falls is not small and the spread of these doubts is worldwide. As an illustration, during the Greek public accounts fraud, the government revised its public deficit forecasts in 2009 from 3.7 points to 12.5 points of gross domestic product (Ernoult, 2012). Despite this climate of doubt and uncertainty regarding auditing, several authors (Manita & Chemangui, 2007; Troi, 2018; Jurakulovna & Bahodirovich, 2021) remain optimistic and still consider auditing to be a guarantor and proof of the quality of financial information. For these authors, audit activity is likely to mitigate the effects of informational asymmetry (Abad et al., 2017). Indeed, the audit seems to be a valid and structured mechanism to establish a climate of trust between shareholders and managers. Moreover, studies conducted by, Mihret et al. (2010), Newman and comfort (2018), and Rahman et al., (2019) have consolidated this view by linking the audit function with possible or achieved performance.

Audit and internal control must contribute to the creation and preservation of the added value of organizations. The control of risks of various types and sizes is a key element in the creation of value. It requires cohesion between teams and standardization of procedures. Internal audit is an autonomous and objective activity. Its ultimate function is to manage the business and add value (Lee et al., 2021). To this end, internal auditing will assess the consistency of objectives, readiness and feasibility, improvement of resources, compliance with instructions and standards, directives and laws, compliance with authorities and hierarchical norms, and ultimately the direction and assets of the organization.

Originally, internal auditing was built around the accounting cycle. Its basic purpose was primarily to complement, anticipate, or consolidate the external audit of financial statements (Chun, 1997). Subsequently, internal auditing has encompassed the other cycles by opening up to complementary areas such as purchasing, customers and suppliers, treasury, etc. The amplification of crises and scandals has developed the need to study risk management, internal control, and corporate governance (Castanheira et al., 2010). This has pushed organizations to assort the possible audit mechanisms by altering external and internal audits. Also, it has favored the emergence of detailed operational audits of cycles like the audit of the cash cycle.

The current orientations and the different crises have propelled the treasury as a particular resource. Financial flexibility is sought after and companies must constantly guarantee the solvency and liquidity of their accounts. At the same time, the treasury function is confronted with several types of varied and related risks. A company's cash position is the total amount of available liquidity. Treasury departments are considered an integral part of the organizations' operations, with tasks as varied as fundraising, cash management, and the implementation of consistent risk management programs (Helliar & Dunne, 2004). The main objective of the treasury function is to optimize financial resources and analyze risks. Therefore, Treasury management revolves around managing these two major levels, liquidity, and financial risks. As a result, cash management is a managerial orientation that aims to guarantee an acceptable level of indebtedness, seize monetary and financial opportunities, and control risks.

The treasury function is of paramount importance to businesses and other organizational forms (Phillot, 2021). Currently, the function and mission of the treasurer have evolved significantly (Polak et al., 2011). This cash flow management involves the daily matching of cash and financial assets to maintain monetary and financial objectives. It is a trade-off between financial and monetary resources and short and long-term uses of investment and operating cycles. The management of flows must be seen as a global task (Bentalha & Hmioui, 2021), which involves the management of long-term financial flows (financing and investment) and also short-term monetary flows (operations). Thus, the management of cash receipts and disbursements is a daily task for companies. Funds must flow quickly and efficiently within firms and with different stakeholders (Hmioui et al., 2018). These funds require periodic and meticulous review. Therefore, it is a competitive factor for any organizational entity (Bragg, 2010).

Thus, the internal audit of the treasury seems to be an element of steering performance and competitiveness. Therefore, an audit of the cash cycle is a basic activity of the auditor whose mission is to gauge compliance with payment and collection standards and also to keep a faithful trace of the operations performed. The aim is to ensure that the various accounting and financial statements, both internal and external, faithfully reflect liquidity operations and that the expenses, revenues, and financial assets related to the cash cycle allow the reader of financial information to make a relevant judgment.

Studies in management science, and in particular in internal control, use very divergent methodological approaches (Koenig, 1993). What we propose in this work is a homogeneous conceptualization of an audit mechanism for the cash cycle. We will begin our analysis with a thorough theoretical development to mobilize the methods and paradigms necessary for our work. Empirical data will be collected through personal interviews and direct observations, as we have conducted internal audits in several companies, and we will analyze documents and management in their actual context to understand the emergence and evolution of certain phenomena. Therefore, the approach that will be used is qualitative. These data provide rich, in-depth, and diversified information (Alla et al., 2020). They are based on experiences, testimonies, and empirical cases. In addition, our approach will be based on a possible case study, supplemented by additional confirmatory case studies. Based on this review, we will propose an empirical approach to the internal audit of the treasury function.

The interest of this work is to provide the company with the methodical and rational means to understand the merits of internal audits. Our vision is to convince them to no longer see the auditors as controllers or reporters, but as collaborators who act in the interest of the company and its executives. Thus, through their advice and recommendations company to create more added value, thus qualifying it for better performance and competitiveness. Also, we believe that with this work, we can allow the managers to see the insufficiencies until now globally unknown in cash management and contribute to the improvement, even the optimization of this cash.

At the theoretical level, our work targets a particular cycle of the company, that of cash flow. Indeed, the audit of the cash flow is a relatively unexplored field of study, because there are few studies on this topic. At the methodological level, our approach will use diversified and complementary approaches. This set of tools aims to give originality to our book and allow the design of practical sheets of internal audit characterized by a high level of comprehensiveness and transversality.

The book is divided into two parts. In the first part, we cover the different conceptual and theoretical notions of internal audit, treasury, and internal audit of the treasury. In the second part, we cover the empirical part of treasury internal auditing by proposing a comprehensive and integrated model of internal auditing of the treasury function.

Internal Audit of Treasury and cash management

Part One:

The theoretical framework of the internal audit of the cash cycle

Internal Audit of Treasury and cash management

CHAPTER 1
THEORETICAL AND CONCEPTUAL APPROACHES TO INTERNAL AUDITING

There are several structural changes in the current economic sphere. The organizational fabric is highly divergent in terms of structure, size, level, and activities of organizational entities. Business enterprises also have several purposes and objectives. Like cells of a living being (Von Bertalanaffy, 1991), businesses exchange with the environment several flows of goods and services, informational flows, and financial flows (Bentalha et al., 2019; Hmioui et al., 2020). These flows require appropriate management to survive and guarantee the sustainability of these organizations.

The development and survival of a company depend on its continuous and progressive capacity to adapt to the changes and complexities of economic, cultural, technological, and social transformations. It is a question of creating steering mechanisms based on forecasting and reactivity while relying on the learning and flexibility of the organization. To face challenges and reach objectives, managers need efficient and up-to-date information and communication tools.

The recent and repeated financial scandals and the collapse of the Andersen firm have created a state of ambiguity and a certain amount of doubt about the place and quality of an audit and account certification mission. Despite this crisis of confidence, several authors (Manita & Chemangui, 2007; Gold & Heilmann, 2019) believe that the auditor remains a guarantor of the quality of financial information and helps to reduce the information asymmetry between shareholders and managers to create value for the various stakeholders. At this level, internal auditing seems to be a modern tool to assess risks and anticipate changes (Pérez-Cornejo et al., 2019). Unlike the traditional functions (purchase, sales, production, personnel, etc.) that originate with the creation of the company and are imposed beforehand, in the beginning, to its management, the internal audit is a support activity and assistance to the management body. It comes to consolidating and completing the other basic functions with qualified personnel based on a standardized methodology and specific deontology (Carcary, 2020). It is an example of a support activity that supports the other core activities. The mission of this activity is to assess the effectiveness and relevance of the internal control system and to make any possible proposals for its improvement. This control system is a process designed to recognize potential incidents that may affect the entity and also to address risks within the limits of its aversion. It is intended to provide reasonable confidence that the organization's objectives will be achieved (IFACI, 2005).

A) Definitions and evolution of internal auditing

The audit is a methodical, independent, and documented process. Its main objective is the recovery of evidence and the evaluation in an objective way to determine to what extent the prerequisite audit criteria are met (ISO 9000). It is an evaluation of the processes of the activity of a company, an association, or a community. It is also an audit of the accounts of a company to ensure that they have been established according to the standards in force. It is also a question of judging the possibilities of errors or omissions that may alter the true and fair view. It is about confirming that the financial statements of companies reflect the economic reality of the company for the different stakeholders. This definition of the audit commits this activity as partial responsibility for the achievement of the objectives set. For this purpose, the auditor has a systematic and standardized activity directed at evaluating the success of the management processes of the organization.

The audit can be divided into two main categories: internal and external. The internal audit is not mandatory. It can be conducted to examine operational activities following a request from management. The main task of the internal auditor is to observe and discuss with the actors involved to evaluate their working methods. He or she may identify changes that could improve productivity or ensure that the various existing procedures are being followed. In addition to this essential task, the internal auditor may also carry out organizational and financial audits to detect possible shortcomings. In contrast, the external audit is mandatory and laid down by law. It is initiated by the legal texts or the shareholders. The external auditor is an independent agent who can work successively or alternatively for several companies.

Internal auditing is an activity that provides an organization with assurance on the level of control of its operations. It serves to support the management of a company or an activity in achieving its objectives by assessing management processes, existing or probable risks, and control and governance mechanisms. The internal auditor can make proposals to strengthen the effectiveness of organizational steering mechanisms. He also provides advice to improve performance and contribute to creating added value. It also seeks to improve the organizational training of the people in the company in the execution of their respective functions effectively and efficiently. It provides analysis, evaluation, recommendations, and information about activities and delivery mechanisms. It may involve all functions of the company or other organizational forms.

The first definition of internal auditing was approved by the Board of Directors of the Institute of Internal Auditors (IIA) on July 15, 1947, and published as part of the "Statement of Responsibilities of Internal Auditing": "Internal auditing is an independent appraisal activity within an organization for the review of accounting, financial, and other operations constituting a basis for protective and constructive services to management. It is a type of control that operates by measuring and evaluating the effectiveness of other types of control. It is primarily concerned with accounting and financial aspects, but it may also be concerned with matters of an operational nature.

"Internal auditing is an independent and objective activity that assures the degree of control over an organization's operations, advises on how to improve them, and contributes to the creation of value. It helps an organization achieve its objectives by systematically and methodically evaluating its risk management, control, and governance processes and making recommendations to improve their effectiveness. (IIA, Institute of Internal Auditors, 1999).

Internal auditing is therefore an autonomous and objective activity that provides an organizational entity with assurance on the degree of control of its operations, provides advice on reforming them, and participates actively and effectively in creating added value. It continually assists the organization in achieving its objectives by systematically and methodically evaluating its risk management, control, and governance processes and making proposals to enhance their effectiveness (IIA, 2000).

It is an independent, global, and neutral activity whose objective is participation in the creation of value through the control of operations and the improvement of procedures (Hmioui et al., 2018). Internal audit also refers to the department located within a company that monitors the effectiveness of its processes and controls.

Internal auditing is not an exclusive activity for companies. This transversal function can be used in any organizational form. Also, the internal audit function does not need a particular structure and adapts to the different organizational forms (large company, small company, administration, association, etc.). Within any organizational form, it is possible to set up an internal audit procedure regardless of the department involved. Nevertheless, the procedures implemented by the internal audit are not fixed but must be adapted and contingent on the possible diversities between the multiple organizational forms.

The internal audit has several indispensable missions:
- Promote and develop value creation for all stakeholders,
- Improve the organization's management processes,
- To make processes and methods more efficient,
- Participate in the control of assets and property,
- Comply with legal regulations and internal guidelines,
- Verify the veracity of information and the ability of information systems to transmit relevant information quickly and efficiently to decision-makers,
- Present possible improvements and progressions,
- Encourage the organization to control risks efficiently and cost-effectively.

Internal auditing is far from being a new activity. Its historical origins go back quite far in economic history. As early as the third century BC, Roman governments hired administrators whose mission was to control the accounting of the provinces. Since that time and the time of the "auditors" of Edward I of England, examples are numerous. For some authors, such as Renard (2006), internal audit, in the modern sense, has a genesis that dates back to the economic crisis of 1929 in the United States. At that time, companies were greatly affected by the economic recession and large American companies sought the help of external audit firms. These origins of auditing are pronounced by accounting historian Richard Brown (1905, cited in Mautz & Sharaf, 1961): "The origin of auditing goes back to times scarcely less remote than that of accounting...Whenever the advance of civilization brought about the necessity of one man being entrusted to some extent with the property of another, the advisability of some kind of check upon the fidelity of the former would become apparent."

Regarding the theoretical foundations of internal auditing, it has long been considered to find its legitimacy in the agency theory. According to this theory, the complexity of today's organizations has changed the power relationships: the "principal" owner loses relative contact with the management of his organization. Knowledge of the potential conflicts that may arise between them can help reduce the costs of eliminating them. It is the shareholder who no longer has the means or the capacity to manage directly. According to Jensen & Meckling (1976), the operational managers (agents) have more information than the shareholder (principals). Although the external auditors guarantee the stockholders the value of the financial reports, it is the independent internal audit function that comforts the board. In this context, this theory is a valid theoretical basis for clarifying the position of the internal auditor. The theory offers a valid mechanism to explain the problems of information asymmetry. It provides an explanation of the missions and roles assigned to an internal auditor that goes far beyond the simple assertion that there is an internal auditor in the company (Adams, 1994).

In bureaucratic theory, order and hierarchy are two important concepts. In contrast to classical and neoclassical economics, behavioral economics provides a way of thinking about how agents make decisions and what influences them (Camerer, 1999). It uses psychology (cognitive and social) and anthropology (Śliwowski & Wincewicz-Price, 2019). An organizational entity is thus understood as several individuals with varying goals and requirements. Thus, the objectives of individuals and groups do not necessarily coincide with those of the organization. For this reason, it is important to verify the harmony of the objectives through an internal audit.

Institutional theories serve primarily as a basis for examining organizational phenomena embedded in broad social, political, and economic environments (Mihret et al., 2010). More importantly, they can provide insight into the practices of internal auditing as a component of organizational systems and shed light on the relationship between internal auditing and the achievement of corporate goals. From the internal auditor's perspective, the organization must conduct a sequential search for satisfactory solutions and possible alternatives. The control structures stipulate the existence of an internal audit capable of verifying compliance with the standards. The decisions made can become routine and this creates mechanisms of standardization (Przybylska & Kańduła, 2019). Knowledge of these motivations and theoretical factors is crucial in the auditor's work since the knowledge and techniques mobilized in the auditing process must be processed with the context and theoretical data in mind.

Currently, internal auditing has undergone a remarkable development marked by a triple orientation: first, in its object (from an internal audit of regularity to an internal audit that aims at performance), then in its objectives (from an internal audit of detection of anomalies and search for fraud to a global internal audit that aims at the critical evaluation of processes and corporate governance), finally, in its sectors of activity and its fields of application (from the exclusivity of internal audit to a private sector ç an extension to the public sector and other organizational forms) The development of skills and the professionalization of internal auditing required the creation of an international body capable of federating the players. Thus, the Institute of Internal Auditors (IIA) was created in 1941 in the United States.

The objective of internal auditing is to help the members of the organization to accomplish their tasks effectively and efficiently. In doing so, internal auditing provides analysis and evaluation of the activities, processes, and operations being audited.

Thus, there is a three-level hierarchy of internal audit objectives (Vatier, 1989):
The first objective of regularity. This involves validating that the audited organizations follow the legal provisions, and the internal standards adopted and that the internal control system is operational and effective. The second objective of the internal audit is related to the efficiency of the audited organization. This involves verifying the quality of the controls performed and the ability of these controls to guide performance. Finally, the third objective of the internal audit is related to relevance. The internal audit aims to ensure that the agreed objectives are in line with the resources committed. It is a continuous concordance between the choices made and the means used.

B)   Types of internal audit missions

We can divide internal auditing assignments into two main categories: assurance and consulting. These two types of missions differ greatly in terms of the objectives pursued and the possible targets. The assurance audit aims to assure the general manager or the members of the board of directors. It, therefore, provides a certain assurance regarding the operations and risks of an organization. It is therefore a neutral and impartial examination of evidence to assess processes, management, and risks. Internal auditors are guarantors of the performance generated because their work is aimed at the sustainability of this added value. Consulting audits are specific to a particular operational function. The consulting activity is related to possible improvement paths and changes. It is therefore a consulting service aimed at creating value and improving processes.

Internal auditing can also be divided into a strategic or operational audit. An operational audit is specific to a particular function and aims primarily to evaluate the adequacy of functional decisions with the overall strategy and objectives. Operational or efficiency audits can be considered for all company functions (Bécour & Bouqui, 2008). This type of internal audit mission provides an overall and synthetic view of the functioning of an assortment of operations or activities. It is also a procedural audit to ensure that the strategic process outlined is followed. It is especially useful for large companies and multinational firms. The strategic audit is aimed at the decision-making center and the top management. Its main purpose is to evaluate the relevance of the goals and strategies chosen according to the context and the means. This exercise is usually followed by a reflection on the risks or possible inconsistencies.

C) The characteristics of internal auditing

Internal auditing has several characteristics. First, it is a separate activity. IIA Standard 1210 states that the chief audit executive must obtain the advice and support of qualified persons with the expertise and other skills necessary to perform all or part of their duties. If the person present does not have the necessary or adequate skills, they may be assisted by advisors and additional assistance. There are no concessions to be made in internal auditing in terms of the necessary skills or know-how. It is an activity in its own right and not a simple task that can be delegated to an operator without experience or adequate training. Indeed, it is a standardized and precise activity that leaves no room for arbitrariness or chance.

The same internal auditing standard specifies the importance of internal auditors having sufficient knowledge and skills to assess risks and anomalies. They must also have a valid understanding of the technological, technical, and information technology risks related to the engagement performed (Pickett, 2000). In this sense, any internal audit engagement that is not within a team's competence, that does not follow the audit guidelines, or that the internal audit team deems beyond their competence or area of expertise must be declined in advance, either at the outset of the engagement or after taking into account new information that changes the prior sense of competence. This is to preserve the professional character of internal auditing (Seol et al., 2011).

Secondly, the internal audit aims to assure the level of control of operations. In the context of an assurance mission, the internal auditor is compulsory to precise a personal opinion on the degree of control of a situation, a system, a function, a process, etc. He, therefore, determines beforehand the nature and scope of his mission, which normally includes three types of participants: the person, department, or procedure to be audited, the auditor, and the user of the audit report. For this reason, the adequacy of the resources deployed should be verified against the objectives.

Internal auditing is an engagement performed at the request of the company's management. Its objective is to assist the client in achieving its objectives. It is therefore a consulting mission capable of adding value. It is the managers requesting the audit mission who choose the scope and role of the auditors' powers. They choose the scope of the study with the auditors and outline the objectives assigned to each mission. This may include consulting, advice, facilitation, process design, or training.

Also, an internal audit aims to create value for stakeholders. To achieve this, it is essential to make this objective concrete and consolidate it with reliable risk management information. The internal auditor's advice should be a benefit and an element of value creation.

Finally, the internal auditor must ensure the effectiveness of control. It encompasses the activities of directing, controlling, and verifying the operations performed. According to the traditional approach, internal control is defined as the set of provisions included in organizations and procedures, the purpose of which is to ensure the quality of information, the protection of assets, compliance with laws as well as with the plans and policies of general management, and the efficiency of the company's operations (Barbier, 1995). Any entity normally has internal control that is intrinsic or inherent to the activity. The extent and control of this control depend on the ability to manage change and organizational learning. The control of risks in the audited entity cannot be accomplished without the support of an effective internal control system. In fact, according to the 2130 standard, the internal audit aims to help the organization maintain an adequate control process by continuously evaluating its effectiveness and efficiency and by encouraging its continuous improvement.

D) Internal auditing standards

Internal auditing standards are organized and categorized in an international framework of professional practice. This framework is promulgated by the IIA. It is a set of guidelines and recommendations for internal auditors around the world. In addition to this framework, the internal auditor can rely on the internal audit charter. It is a report that includes the audit process, particularly the nature of reports, authorizes access to documents, relations with personnel, and the means necessary to carry out internal auditing assignments. It is therefore a definition of the scope of internal audit activities.

The purpose of the Standards for Internal Auditing is (IIA, 2015):
1. To guide the application of the compulsory elements of the International Professional Practices Framework for Internal Auditing;
2. Develop a value-added approach to internal auditing activities;
3. Establish criteria for evaluating internal auditing;
4. Drive improvements in the organization's operations and procedures.

The Internal Auditing Standards are classified using a system of numbers and letters. The names also distinguish between the Qualification Standards (1000 series) and the Operating Standards (2000 series). The Implementation Standards have an "A" if they relate to assurance activities, and a "C" if they relate to consulting activities.

▶ Qualification Standards:
The qualification standards (1000 series) outline and explain the skills and qualifications required for an internal auditor. They consist of three main sections.

◈ Missions, Powers, and Resistibilities (1000): The mission of the internal auditor must be set in advance and explained as part of the audit charter.

◈ Independence and objectivity (1100): the mission of the internal auditor must be inscribed in a posture of autonomy and sovereignty and the internal auditors must perform their work with objectivity and impartiality. "A calling requiring specialized knowledge and often long and intensive preparation including instruction in skills and methods as well as scholarly principles underlying the skills and methods, maintaining by force of organization or concerted opinion, high standards of achievement and conduct and committing its members to continued study and to a kind of work which has for its prime purpose the rendering of a public service." (IAA, 2001).

Independence is persuaded as the scarcity and absence of significant conflicts of interest or separation of powers that threaten objectivity and fairness, while objectivity is defined as a state of mind or mental state in which biases and presumptions do not affect assessments, judgments, and verdicts in an inward and unhealthy manner (Mutchler, 2003).

- Independence

Having independence in internal auditing is crucial. This means that the auditor has all the conditions to perform the task fairly and impartially. For Mutchler et al (2001) independence in internal auditing can be defined as: "freedom from material conflicts of interest that threaten objectivity. In other words, it is a state where threats to objectivity are managed to the extent that the risks of ineffective internal audit services are acceptably controlled". It involves access to information and the opportunity to discuss with board members. It also involves the ability to demonstrate that there are no conflicts of interest or likely incompatibilities in the internal audit engagement.

The list of threats to the independence of the internal auditor is relatively long (Christopher et al., 2009). The first threat is the attitude of some managers to use the internal audit function as a training ground. This involves taking a small team and training them in management and control techniques under the guise of having an internal audit committee. This amounts to considering internal audits as a springboard for future managers. This choice leads to a blurring of objectivity and independence, and auditors will quickly become subservient to people who can control or shape the future development of their professional careers. The second threat to independence considers budget approval and the financial needs of internal audit. This involves placing technical or financial constraints on the auditor's mission or diminishing the scope and impact of the agreed-upon audit engagement. The third threat relates to the role assigned to senior management in the design or validation of the internal audit plan. If internal auditors accept management's interference, they will be viewed as consultants. This situation will be detrimental to the independence of the internal audit function, both in terms of the work they perform and in terms of their image within the organization. The fourth threat concerns the possible mismatch between prescribed methods and field applications by auditors. Indeed, internal auditing is by definition a methodical and standardized activity. It assumes a meticulous follow-up of certain methodological approaches. The fifth threat that internal auditors must face is related to the composition and rank of these auditors. Indeed, the possibility of the presence of unqualified people or people with high-ranking positions could harm the objectivity of the audit mission. The sixth and final threat to independence relates to the possibility of appointing, removing, or changing the mandate of internal auditors. This threat is also significant even if senior management can evaluate the internal audit function.

On the other hand, several procedures consolidate the independence of the internal auditor. First, the internal audit charter and the acceptance of the internal audit plan, the resource plan, and the budgets must be established in advance. These different documents show the place and importance of the internal auditor's mission. Also, there is the possibility to follow the communications of the head of internal audit and to ratify the appointments and possible dismissals of the internal audit team. It also can set the remuneration of the internal audit team in advance and clarify the limitations of the scope of the internal audit or the resources.

- Objectivity

Objectivity is an unbiased and fair mental attitude. It is a primary requirement in the auditor's profession. It enables auditors to perform assignments with a minimum assurance on the quality of the work. It requires that internal auditors focus on the tasks personally and do not submit their judgment on audit tests and issues to others.

There are several alternative conditions for objectivity. To be impartial requires that the internal auditor personally performs the agreed-upon tasks. In some cases, the internal auditor can be queried to provide supplementary and complementary duties and responsibilities. Thus, the absence of conflicts of interest or multiple engagements is conducive to justifying the auditor's independence.

At the individual level, there are several threats to an internal auditor's objectivity (Stewart & Subramaniam, 2010). The first is self-examination, characterized by the auditor's duality of audit engagement and audit control. These two functions should normally be separated and performed by different teams. Secondly, there is the possibility of the existence of social pressure characterized by physical, monetary, or psychological constraints exerted on the internal auditor. Also, the presence of economic self-interest may hinder the internal auditor's mission. This type of problem occurs when the auditor has a personal interest in the outcome. For example, incentive benefits for a successful audit or the possibility of promotion to another position with greater responsibility after the audit engagement. Also, the presence of personal relationships can hinder the objectivity of internal audit engagement. This is the presence of affiliation, friendship, or kinship between internal auditors and members of the audited entity's management. Also, familiarity ensuing from an enduring association with the audited entity may impair the auditor's objectivity. This is the case, for example, of having worked for a long time with the administrative team or in the audited department. Finally, there are cultural, racial, and gender biases that arise in transnational organizations when the auditor is influenced or does not understand the resident ethos and civilizations.

❖ Competence and Awareness (1200): Competence provides an understanding of the content, capabilities, and other values that internal auditors need to perform their professional duties effectively. It covers awareness of required functions, patterns, and developing topics to enable appropriate guidance and advice. It is a matter of having a set of qualifications or certificates related to the area of expertise being audited and also have years of experience at the national or international level. Certificates of complementary training or online training are also advisable, especially if they come from certified and recognized organizations. For example, the Certified Internal Auditor designation obtainable by the IIA and other dedicated organizations can confirm the auditor's competence.

Seol et al. (2011) distinguished five broad families of skills required by the internal auditor:
- Factor loadings for Technical skills (Using information technology, Spreadsheets, Communication, Statistical methods, and theories of organizational control);
- Factor loadings for Analytic/Design skills (Logical mental, Aptitude to conceptualize, Problem analysis, Research skills, using data, Linking evidence to arguments and conclusions)
- Factor loadings for Appreciative skills (Distinguishing position of data, Organization out the relevant, arbitrating whether material is adequate, Vigilant, accommodating of original, to improve continuously)
- Factor loadings for Personal skills (Honor, Integrity, Critical thinking, Well-balanced, Enterprising, Smart, Flexible, can adapt to changing circumstances, Change in self, Goal-oriented, Friendly, Trusting, Eager, Accept responsibility)
- Factor loadings for Interpersonal skills (Communication, Presentation skills, Managing frustration, Discretion, Empathy, Diplomacy, Supportive of others, Culture sensitivity)

❖ **Quality Assurance and Improvement Program (1300):** The quality assurance and improvement program must be designed and periodically updated. This must support and encompass central elements in the internal audit mission. It is therefore a comprehensive and coherent document. Its primary purpose is to provide an assessment of the compliance of the audit engagement with the selected standards. It is also a tool for verifying compliance with internal auditors' codes of ethics. It must also allow for frequent updates to make it compatible with structural or strategic changes.

➤ Operating Standards (2000 series): These standards document and explain the contours of internal auditing engagements and determine validity criteria.

- Planning (2010): It reflects the professionalism of the auditor. It is therefore a prepared and standardized exercise and far from being an improvised task. This demonstrates the professional nature of the audit, which distinguishes it from activities for beginners.
- Communication and approval (2020): It is an imperative rule to communicate among the audit team and also to communicate with other stakeholders and management.
- Resource Management (2030): This involves managing material, monetary, informational, and managerial resources. This principle also confirms the professional nature of internal auditing. Indeed, an audit mission cannot be improvised and therefore requires efficiently deployed resources.
- Rules and Procedures (2040): The procedures established are related to the complexity and scope of the internal audit work required.
- Coordination and Reliability (2050): Explain information, link tasks, and ensure adequate coverage. One must understand the requested study and link the different components.
- Reporting to the Board and Senior Management (2060): The reports are set about the management and the board. It is not a question of establishing a large number of reports but rather of setting up adequate communication with the needs and contexts.

◆ Nature of work (2100)

The work of the internal auditor is centered on the evaluation of processes and the continuous improvement of the company's operations. It manages the business activities of the company's management by targeting the monitoring of risks and control mechanisms.

The internal audit activity requires a continuous assessment and follow-up of appropriate recommendations to improve the governance processes to:
- Make decisions.
- Oversee risk management and control.
- Promote appropriate ethics and values.
- Ensure effective management of organizational performance and accountability.
- Communicate risk and control information.
- Coordinate and communicate with the Board of Directors, external and internal auditors, other insurance providers, and management.

◆ Engagement Planning (2200)
Internal audit engagement involves planning through an engagement plan. This plan includes the objectives, scope, schedule, and resources required. It should group the objectives and risks of the engagement.

◆ Mission Completion (2300)
Internal auditors must perform the engagement with the established methodologies and agreed-upon schedules. This primarily involves identifying, evaluating, and documenting the information necessary to achieve the objectives.

◆ Communication of Results (2400)
Communicating the results of the study is among the priorities for internal auditors. This involves presenting the objectives, scopes, conclusions, recommendations, and proposed action plans. The style of this communication should be professional and direct. The communication should be clear and easily understood.

◆ Monitoring Progress Actions (2500)
The chief audit executive must establish and maintain, a system for monitoring the follow-up of results reported to management.

◆ Management's Acceptance of Risk (2600)
When it is determined that management has accepted a risk that is deemed unacceptable, the matter should be reviewed with

management. In the event of continuing disagreement, the auditor should inform the Board of Directors.

E) Competencies of the internal auditor

Internal auditing standards are restrictive. To be able to validate these standards, the internal auditor must have several skills and knowledge. Internal auditors are expected to apply and adhere to the following principles (as defined in the IIA Standards for Internal Auditing and Code of Ethics):

- Integrity: Integrity is about building trust between the auditors and the members of the organization. It is to perform the tasks honestly, to respect the law, to have a legal activity not incompatible with the mission of the audit, and to contribute to the ethical and moral rules.
- Objectivity: Objectivity reflects a standardized and balanced assessment. It means not having a conflict of interest, not accepting assignments that may compromise the objective evaluation, and maintaining professional confidentiality.
- Confidentiality - This includes adhering to the terms of confidentiality. This includes protecting information and being professional in the use of actionable information by the organization's objectives and ethics.
- Competence - Internal auditors use knowledge and skills to achieve assigned objectives. This includes taking on assignments in their areas of expertise, providing services by standards, and continuously improving their skills.

F) Internal audit as a risk management tool

The internal auditor must assess the relative effectiveness of risk management processes and also participate in their improvement while refraining from assuming operational responsibility for them (IFACI, 2009). Theoretically, risk can be defined as a possible event whose actual occurrence is likely to cause significant damage to the organization. The Federation of European Risk Management Associations defines risk management as "a process by which organizations address the risks associated with their activities and thereby seek sustainable benefits from those activities. Risk can therefore be related to exposure to a potential hazard, inherent in a situation or activity (de Zwaan et al., 2011; Hmioui et al., 2018). If not detected and managed effectively, it can have a systemic occurrence and negative impacts giving more ongoing inconvenience to the organization. Eventually, it can even create a global dysfunction in the entity. Any act of entrepreneurship already involves a significant degree of risk and this creates a specificity of the managerial decision marked by the omnipresence of risk.

From the auditor's point of view, risk factors that can lead to adverse consequences are considered organizational deficiencies and should be taken into consideration in any due diligence process. For example, reading previous audit reports is one of the desirable steps in any auditor's assignment. The study of risks is therefore a necessary and fundamental step for any internal audit because it must assess the risk factors that may have financial or social consequences or examine the failings of the organization and encourage the occurrence of an event.

There are many types of risk. We will limit our analysis by classifying them into two basic categories by origin and by nature.

The origin of the risks expresses the starting point of risk and the place of its creation. It can be either internal or external. The following table summarizes these two approaches.

Table 1: Internal and external sources of risk

Internal risks		External risks	
Linked to the organization	Lack of formalized standards and procedures	Stakeholders	Customers	Cessation of payment of a major customer
	Lack of steering tools		Suppliers	Non-conformity of supplies
	Failure to address safety concerns		Service providers	Errors of appreciation
Related to human resources	Undefined responsibilities		Intermediates	Misunderstanding of needs
	Competencies deficiencies		Public organizations	Tax Adjustment
Linked to information systems	System failure	Market conditions	Concurrence	Acquisition of a competitor by a global group
			Technological advances	High cost
	Hacking of sensitive data		Economic conditions	Rising interest rates
			Political situation	Pension Reform
		Legislative changes	Environmental Law	High cost

Source: adapted from El Menzhi (2011, p. 209)

In the second typology, risks can be classified by their respective natures. We then speak of speculative, random, or mixed risks. The following table summarizes this type of risk.

Table 2: Risks by nature

Risk		Examples of events that can generate risks for the organization
Speculative or entrepreneurial risk	Dependent on the quality and relevance of the decisions made by the manager during his or her management (a strategic decision that may result in a gain or loss)	management in the hands of a single person, without a committee or supervisory board
		An organization whose complex structure does not seem justified
		major internal control deficiencies are systematically overlooked when they could be corrected high turnover of accounting and financial managers
		frequent changes in legal counsel or auditors
Random or pure risks	Occur unexpectedly and abruptly	natural disasters (earthquakes, floods, storms, landslides)
		Accidents (work, transport, fire, air conditioning, heating...)
		Theft of material goods, fraud
		Sabotage of material goods, data, computer programs
Mixed risks	Sudden events related to management (strikes, supplier failures, machine breakdown, etc.)	Transactions with related parties (insider trading, etc.)
		Payments deemed unreasonable about services provided
		purchase at prices significantly above or below market (lack of competition) unusual cash payments

Source: adapted from El Menzhi (2011, p. 211)

The recommended approach to risk management requires identifying risks, assessing them, treating and classifying them, and finally matching the severity of the risks with the implications. For optimal risk management, it is necessary to start by identifying the risks before resolving or preventing them.

A detailed identification of risk is mandatory for the development of a viable enterprise risk monitoring and control system. It would require taking into account both internal (company structure, nature of its activities) and external factors (developments in its industry and technological advances (Bentalha, 2020)) that would have failures on the system and limitations in the face of achieving the objectives (Griffiths, 2016).

Thus, each company should identify the most dangerous risks and also assess their possible vulnerabilities to these risks. Based on the two risk analysis criteria are generally the severity of the risk, which measures the consequences for the company, and the probability of the risk occurring, which determines the rate of occurrence, risks can be prioritized into critical, major, moderate, and minor risks.

Before planning the risk mapping of each company, the internal auditor must establish a risk severity rating scale and a risk probability rating scale (Sinha et al., 2019). To Bernard et al. (2008) "risk mapping is a living steering tool that must allow for regular measurement of the entity's progress in its level of risk control". Also, for Matte (2002) "in the same way that financial statements present the financial situation of an entity, risk mapping presents the image of an organization's risks".

There are several presentations of risk mapping in the economic and managerial literature, but we preferred to use the one presented by Bernard et al. (2010) through the rating scales summarized in Tables 3 and 4.

Table 3: Risk Severity Rating Scale

5	Very significant	Put the balance of the company in question, even its survival
4	Major	Does not really put the company in complete peril, but very serious and must imperatively be treated
3	Moderate	Can only be tolerated at first, as a temporary measure
2	Minor	Has consequences, but can be tolerated
1	Not significant	Without any remarkable consequence

Source: Bernard et al. (2010, p. 66)

The result of the product "severity x probabilities" gives what is called the mathematical expectation of severity or criticality (Bernard et al., 2010).

Table 4: Scale for assessing the likelihood of the risk occurring

5	Almost certain	This will surely happen in the short or medium term
4	Likely	It will certainly happen one day or another
3	Possible	Technically possible
2	Unlikely	It is possible that it could happen one day
1	Rare	It will never happen

Source: Bernard et al. (2010, p. 66)

G) Internal audit and related professions

To better understand the role, responsibilities and mission of ,the internal auditor, it is necessary to present the differences between this profession and related professions:

a) internal and external auditing
The differences between internal and external audits can be summarized as follows (Lemant, 1995; Renard, 2006, 2003).

1) The beginning of the audit mission: The internal auditor begins his or her mission based on an engagement order agreed upon with top management. However, the external auditor is selected by the shareholders' meeting.

2) The status of the auditor: The internal audit is an activity carried out by an employee of the company or an executive, whereas the external audit is entrusted to a chartered accountant who is a member of the Order of Chartered Accountants, an external agent of the company.

3) The nature of the mission: The mission of a public accountant or an external auditor aims at certifying the financial statements and accounts of the company. While the internal audit:
- Does not certify the legality of operations, but assesses that processes are followed and used regularly and that they produce the expected results.
- Evaluates risk management and internal control processes and is

not an audit of accounts, but a diagnosis of operational systems.
- Assures the control of operations and processes by examining the causes of obstacles and by formulating recommendations and advice to introduce improvements in work processes.

4) The methodology used: On the one hand, the external audit begins its activity with the financial results and accounts, provoking a verification while assessing the internal control procedures that led to their composition. On the other hand, the internal audit begins its investigation with an analysis of the objectives and a global appreciation of the risk management processes. The aim is to discover, apprehend and correct dysfunctions that may lead to managerial or financial complications at all levels of the company.

5) Summaries and conclusions of the audit: On the one hand, the external auditor delivers a very succinct report, summarized and oriented towards the certification or not of the accounts or towards certification with reservations. This summary report is intended directly for the board of directors and the general meeting of shareholders. It certifies the accuracy (true and fair view) of the accounting and financial information intended for current or future shareholders, the State, and the general public. On the other hand, the internal auditor gives very detailed reports with justifications and explanations which are intended for the management bodies of the company. The internal audit will issue a detailed opinion on the relevance of the objectives in terms of effectiveness, efficiency, and economy recorded during their achievement. Also, it explains the difficulties, giving the causes and possible recommendations. Depending on the nature of the mission, the internal auditor may certify the compliance of processes and personnel with the company's laws and procedures.

b) Internal audit and management control:

The internal audit has moved from a simple accounting control to the accompaniment of management in the control of risks. Management control has moved from simple cost analysis to budgetary control and then, in a more modern approach, to real steering of the company's performance. Several points of divergence can be identified between these two concepts:

1) The central question studied: The objective of management control is the choice of objectives and the adequacy of these objectives with the adopted budgets and plans. The internal audit, is a question of questioning the method for improving the functioning of the company by examining the processes and recommending solutions to correct the causes of dysfunctions.

2) The objectives pursued: Management control supports the company in choosing its objectives and in steering its activities. The objective is to achieve the objectives set with effectiveness, efficiency, and economy. For its part, the internal audit helps to achieve the objectives by assessing the management processes.

3) The periodicity of the approach: Normally, management control is a permanent activity in companies, whereas the intervention of the internal audit is cyclical and intermittent in time.

4) The methodology used: Management control focuses more on financial information and management indicators (Bentalha, 2022). Its role is to ensure that the company's major variables are maintained by focusing attention on recorded or probable deviations and also by demanding corrective action. The work of the internal auditor aims to improve control of activities by assessing risk management processes.

H) The internal audit approach

Internal auditing must follow a process to be successful. It is a process in which several stages follow one another and which aims to provide the auditor with the elements necessary to issue a reliable opinion. This approach can be summarized in three main phases (Figure 1):

Figure 1: The phases of the internal audit

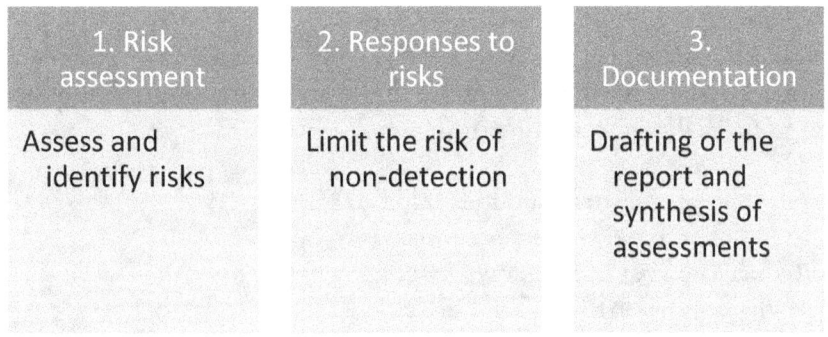

This internal audit process requires three complementary phases:

1) Preparation phase
The audit begins with the preparation phase. This preliminary phase is based on the detection of weaknesses. It, therefore, requires strong reading, attention, and learning skills. It also requires a good knowledge of the company, and the ability to learn quickly and efficiently.

2) Implementation phase
It is at this level that one calls upon the analytical skills and the sense of logic which will enable him to elaborate his audit mission. It requires more observation, dialogue, and, communication skills.

3) Synthesis phase
The auditor must prepare and present his or her report after having gathered all the decisive evidence in the form of a conclusive report

called the "internal audit report".

CHAPTER 2
THE COMPANY'S TREASURY

A. Definition of cash flow (treasury)

The management of financial and monetary flows in companies and other organizational forms is reserved for the treasury function. It encompasses two main components, namely liquidity management and financial risk management (Hubert, 1997).

Cash flow has several functions (Sion, 2001):
- Ensure the liquidity of the company;
- Reduce the cost of banking services;
- Manage short-term financial risks;
- Ensure the security of transactions.

The most important part of cash flow involves having the right amount of money to meet commitments. It is a matter of consolidating the strategies and the daily obligations fixed. According to Meunier (2005), "net cash represents the short-term financing needed by the company to bridge the gap between working capital and working capital requirements". This view of cash flow is more oriented towards immediately available cash (cash in hand and balances in banks). Thus, cash flow is the money supply generated by the continuous operation of a company and therefore reflects its economic and financial health (Hmioui et al., 2018).

According to Sion (2006), "potential cash flow, therefore, represents the net cash and credit reserves and investments available to the firm". Vernimmen et al (2009) state that "cash flow is the difference between the firm's available funds and the current bank loans granted to it". This leads us to conceive of net cash as the difference between cash assets and cash liabilities. According to Hubert (1997), cash flow represents the result of the financial balance between working capital and working capital requirements. The calculation of working capital and working capital requirements leads to the cash balance, hence the relationship:

Net cash = Working capital - Working capital requirements
(functional and financial vision of cash flow).

This same vision is shared by Poloniato and Voyenne (1997). For these authors, the level of working capital and working capital requirements determines the level of the cash surplus or shortfall.

For Depallens and Jobard (1997) "the notion of cash flow can be understood in terms of flows, corresponding to receipts and disbursements during a period". This vision is flow-oriented. Thus, there are two flows in cash flow (Gervais, 1983):
- Receipts: These are receipts, products, loans, subsidies, disposals, capital flows from shareholders, and other resources. These are therefore operations that involve an inflow of money and all the sums that the company will receive over a given period.
- Disbursements: decipher payments of supplier or bank debts, salaries and social expenses, operating expenses, investments, dividends, and other possible disbursements.

To calculate the net cash balance, add the cash receipts for the period to the beginning balance and then subtract the cash disbursements from the beginning balance to get the final cash balance. This gives the following equation:

Beginning cash balance + receipts for the period - disbursements = cash balance

The table that summarizes this relationship is the cash budget.

The treasury function, because of its missions and impacts, plays a very important role in the management of a company (Polak et al., 2020). Cash management is therefore an important issue for company managers and shareholders. Indeed, according to Hubert (1997), the financial stakes of a company's cash flow are measured through a comparison of net income and financial expenses. In addition, cash flow represents the final result of all the balance sheet accounts and is therefore an indicator linked to all the balance sheet and management accounts. In addition, given their liquidity and complexity, cash accounts are sensitive to operational risks.

According to Sion (2001), the treasurer can improve his financial results through several methods. First, he must:
- Plan a daily management procedure to obtain or get as close as possible to "zero cash flow";
- Debate financing conditions by negotiating interest rates, methods of calculating the number of days, and also bank commissions;
- Make rational and methodical cash flow forecasts to make the most profitable financing or investment decisions;
- Reduce costly bank overdrafts and non-interest-bearing bank credit balances;
- Educate management and staff on proper cash flow management.

Hubert (1997) suggests that more attention should be paid to banking terms to reduce the overall cost of the treasury function. This choice is justified by the importance of these banking costs in the overall cost nomenclature of the function.

Several activities are therefore necessary:
- Cash Flow Forecasting
- Working capital control: Review the company's working capital policies.
- Cash concentration: Have a centralized view of cash flow.
- Investments: Use the company's investment policy.
- Granting credit: This involves managing the policy for granting credit conditions.
- Collecting funds:
- Risk management: Use hedging and offsetting strategies to reduce risk.
- Bank Relations: Work with the company's bankers by informing them of financial plans. Also, try to get the best terms from the banks.
- Reporting: Design and provide periodic reports.

- Mergers and acquisitions: Explain the effects of mergers on the cash flow or the group.

For global corporations, the treasury department is tasked with circulating money through the business system and between business units. It must be able to move money between the different components while taking into account the need to keep cash in a centralized system.

B. The components of the treasury function

1. Liquidity management

Liquidity management consists in respecting the solvency of the company, i.e. not to be in default of payment. It is a matter of keeping sufficient liquidity to honor commitments on time. The objective of this Cash Management is to achieve efficient management of cash flows and maximum visibility of them. The correct management of liquidity makes it possible to face situations in which if the cash flow is low, the reconstitution or the increase of its level does not pose a problem.

2. Financial and liquidity risk management

Financial risk management is considered to be the hedging of interest rate and exchange rate risks. The objective is to avoid a high rate, which would then have a damaging effect on the business's profitability.

Aschenbroich et al. (1997) consider that the management of currency and interest rate risks follows the same protection and risk management mechanisms:
• The establishment of a currency rate at a given date, after the current date (forward hedging);
• The possibility of setting a maximum or minimum rate for a currency.

Financial risk management is not limited to simply hedging interest rate and exchange rate risks. Each manipulation made by the treasurer generates financial risks such as signature risks, default risks, counterparty risks, tax risks, and human risks. All of these risks need to be controlled and managed in a forward-looking manner.

C. The objectives of cash management

Managing a cash flow consists of forecasting expenses and revenues. It means anticipating variations and therefore ensuring that the financial means are in place to compensate for these variations. Rousselot & Verdié (2017) state that basic cash management refers to the portion of working capital that is the optimal level needed for a company's cash flow. However, if the profit opportunities offered by the cash flow generation process are to be maximized, this scope must be expanded to include more operational decisions, as optimal cash levels are influenced by other factors outside the restrictive concept of "cash flow."

The primary purpose of cash management is to:
- Maximize the return on excess funds,
- Minimize the cost of funding,
- Improve communication with investors,
- Ensure company liquidity,
- Reduce banking costs.

The goal is to bring cash balances closer to zero. A negative cash balance exposes the company to financial risk and requires the use of expensive equipment to maintain the business. If the balance is very positive, it is profitable to invest these idle resources to generate new profits.

Cash management provides a global view of expenses and resources. One can then:
- Determine funding requirements.
- Forecast future changes in cash flow.
- Monitor developments and activities so you can react as quickly as possible if needed.
- Make the right decisions.
- Coordinate all expenditures with the relevant financial institutions.

Cash flow management thus encompasses several complementary components. Cash flow forecasting and budgeting are very important because they allow the company to maintain short-term liquidity. Any excess cash could be reinvested productively. Encourage prompt payment by customers. This can be done by offering cash discounts for early payments. Early conversion of cash to cash. Once the customer has made payment by issuing a check, collection can be made by promptly cashing the check.

The presence of checks and documents in the treasury is replaced by transfers to the company's accounts. Bank concentration is a useful technique to accelerate the collection of receivables. As an example, the use of digital invoices and e-mail can significantly reduce the waiting time and consequently speed up the entry of money into the company's accounts. Transferring funds from one bank to another electronically can save a lot of time and effort. The company can also use post office boxes in important collection centers.

D. The company treasurer

According to Sion (2001), treasurers must consistently apply procedures and measures to ensure that the company always has the resources to meet its obligations. Corporate treasurers are responsible for assessing and protecting a company from financial risks that may result from its activities. The primary responsibilities of a corporate treasurer are analyzing and monitoring daily cash flow and short-term cash needs, managing investments, making financial investment decisions, funding requirements, managing cash compliance, analyzing markets, and managing cash risks, which may involve managing currency, interest rate, and commodity risks, implementing hedging strategy, valuing financial assets, and managing profitability.

Sion (2001) argues that the treasurer must reduce the cost of banking services through the negotiation of banking terms. To do this, he or she must:
o Establish a detailed inventory of banking conditions;
o Define negotiation priorities (prioritization of objectives);
o Control the negotiated terms (enforcement and compliance).

A corporate treasurer uses internal company information and keeps abreast of external market information and analysis. Treasurers strive to cultivate and maintain good working relationships with key stakeholders in the banking and financial services industries.

There are several possible positions and jobs related to the treasury:
- Financial managers
- Treasury analysts,
- Treasury traders,
- Treasury accountants,
- Risk managers,
- Treasury managers,
- Financial analysts,
- Group treasurers,
- Customer relationship managers,
- Financial directors,
- Financial controllers,
- Small business owners.

The treasurer will have to use several tools and methods. In addition to the cash flow forecast, he or she can use suitable software to manage the cash flow. These are programs that automate calculations and monitor various indicators simultaneously. The software must facilitate the realization of the reports and must allow a consolidated follow-up of the cash flows in real-time.

Thus, to carry out his missions and face the various risks, the company treasurer must have several key skills:
- Ability to adapt,
- Analytical skills,
- Time management,
- Attention to detail,
- Risk management,
- Problem-resolution abilities,
- Communication competencies,
- Strategic decision-making,
- Interpersonal Competencies.

E. Current cash management challenges

Treasury management is currently complex due to the contemporary environment (Bentalha et al., 2021). Digital data, internationalization, and the use of Big-Data provide several new opportunities to evolve the treasury function.

In today's global economy, treasurers must evolve their practices from a function focused on achieving incremental gains in productivity to one that can deliver significant business value. They face a myriad of challenges that they must address.

1. Globalization
As companies continue to expand into new markets, treasury managers face an additional burden to adapt and support rapid growth. The interdependencies and interconnections born of globalization foster the spread of financial risks.

2. Expanding the role
Currently, the treasurer needs to be a mathematician, a software engineer, a financial, and an accounting professional. These different roles require a versatile, flexible, and learning profile.

3. Security
The security and predictability of cash flow are prerequisites for the serenity of business management. In our context, the risk of fraud and cybercrime is significantly increased.

4. Regulation
The regulation of cash flow requires more transparency of activities and processes.
☐
As such, cash flow is one of the most critical factors in determining a company's survival. For these and other reasons, cash flow is a key area of focus for auditors.

CHAPTER 3
INTERNAL AUDIT OF THE TREASURY CYCLE

Every day, companies are exposed to different types of risks, including the risk of bankruptcy and default. At the operational execution level, there are daily cash flows that carry risks and require special attention. The objective of cash management is to manage these risks. The introduction of an internal audit focused on the finance department is therefore of great interest to many companies.

A)   Objectives of the audit of treasury operations

A cash flow audit does not differ greatly from other forms of audit. Its main purpose is to safeguard the company's monetary and financial resources against various risks.

The mass of processing and the complexity of internal or external circuits lead to the following risks
- External fraud or internal takeover.
- Technical problems that may occur in the system.
- Use of payment instruments for money laundering purposes.

To face these different risks, the internal audit of the treasury cycle is divided into two levels: the disbursement level and the collection level.

Concerning payments

- Ensure that payments are accounted for.
- Monitor how costs are assessed.
- Review segregation of duties, especially when dealing with various instances of non-compliance.
- Verify the legality of each payment by documenting and verifying relevant accounting records.
- Ensure that payments, which have already been accounted for and stored, actually correspond to expenses related to the company's daily

operations and activities.

Concerning cash receipt

- Ensure that all revenues are recorded in the correct accounting period and correspond to actual revenues.
- Ensure segregation of duties, particularly in handling various instances of non-compliance.
- Ensure the recording of revenues and the method of allocation and valuation of those revenues.

B) Delineation of auditable cash cycle transactions

The company's cash flow requires an audit to provide an opinion on the regularity, fairness, and fair and objective presentation of the financial statements. The objective of this audit is to establish and confirm that the transactions comply with the pre-established rules and that there are no major risks in this operational cycle.

To this end, a methodology is first adopted to evaluate the internal control system. Given a large number of transactions and the limited time available for the audit mission, it is necessary to distinguish and categorize the transactions. The scope of the audit program for the cash cycle (bank and treasury) depends on the extent to which the auditor relies on the recommended approach.

a) Payment control

Companies tend to make payments by bank (checks or transfers) or by draft, as this method of settlement provides more security for the movement of funds and is easier for companies to control (Hmioui et al., 2021). Therefore, proper internal control reduces cash payments (advances on expenses, small transport costs, cash vouchers, etc.) to the minimum possible.

1) Payments by check or bank transfer

Today, most payments in businesses are made by check. In the U.S., legislation encouraged the development of payment by check (Quinn & Roberds, 2008). The advantage of this practice is due to the tax restrictions and control that this method of payment offers. Amounts deposited in a bank are by definition less accessible and easier to control than cash. In addition, the movement of bank funds can be tracked (accounting information) by a card held by a third party (in this case the bank), which is regularly sent to the company and can be monitored (e.g. by bank statements or other reconciliation methods). Current digital technologies have enabled a rapid shift to electronic transactions (Fatonah et al., 2018).

Even though using checks for settlements to provide security and traceability of transactions, additional internal control procedures must be provided. Thus, several rules are considered for payments by check or wire transfer.

i. Authorized signatures

Normally, a double signature is always required for checks or transfers over a certain amount. In the case of large companies, a third signature may be required if the signatories are absent. The executives who have the power to sign cheques with the banks must be specified in the minutes of the board of directors that give the banks this power.

The signatures should not be connected with the preparation or recording of checks. It is also desirable that they not be able to approve documents authorizing settlement.

ii. Issuance of checks or money orders

Checks made out and presented to signatories must be crossed. Also, these checks must be made out to the payees. The responsibility for their safekeeping rests with the signatories. Under no circumstances should they be returned to the person who prepared them.

iii. Examination, verification, and cancellation of documents

Executives should only cash checks after a thorough review of the attached supporting documentation. These vouchers should be the original verified invoice and the documents bearing these indications. Once the check is issued, these documents must be filed and canceled with a payment indication entered manually or with the help of a special "Paid" stamp or a payment serial number from the company's accounting.

Good internal control should provide:
- That checks presented to signatories are crossed and made out to payees.
- That their retention until they are sent to their recipients is strictly the responsibility of the signatories.
- That they must be sent promptly.

Proper internal control must be in place to avoid double or improper payments. Signatories must be able to review the attached supporting documents, which must be original. The signatories check that the approval procedure by the responsible departments for calculations, prices, quantities delivered, etc., is applied.

2) Payment by cash

i. Principle of cash payment

The fundamental principle in terms of cash payment is that cash receipts received should not be applied directly to the payment of expenses. A cash receipt must be allocated globally to the cash in hand and must not be offset directly. Also, a maximum payment amount per cash register must be stated whether it is daily or monthly.

It is recommended to have a single cash register (per site or per establishment) to facilitate the rules of its operation and thus better guarantee the control operations. In this case, the multiplication of cash registers per lessor should be avoided. Whenever possible, depending on the size of the organization and the volume of transactions processed, the use of the cash box should be limited, as it involves more risks and uncertainties than the use of a bank account.

The cashier must make payments to the bank when the cash reaches a predetermined maximum amount. There should be unannounced checks and periodic cash inventories.

ii. Signatures accepted in cash

It is necessary to establish in advance a special organization of authorizations that must be made by limitedly designated persons. These authorizations may be made by different persons depending on the need to use the cash. These persons must fill out a specific document for these payments.

iii. Examination, Verification, and Cancellation of Documents

The cashier must verify that the vouchers displayed to him/her have been authorized by the officers. He/she must also verify that the amounts used do not exceed the monthly and daily limits.

He/she must verify the identity of the beneficiary. The beneficiary must sign a receipt presented by the Caisse manager, which the latter will keep for future reference.

b) Control of receipts

i. Cashing of checks

Checks must be systematically crossed. They must also include the name of the payee and the date received. The check remittance procedure consists of depositing one or more checks in the bank account.

The cashing of a check is not always followed by the corresponding credit to the account. The most frequent case is that of a bad check, where the account of the issuer of the check does not have sufficient funds, which leads to the rejection by his bank. The bank must promptly inform the check submitter. Thus, it is necessary to put a permanent follow-up of the checks and the realized cashing.

Persons with bank signatures are authorized to endorse checks by signature or stamp.

ii. Cash Receipts

The business must first ensure that it has control over all receipts from cash sales. Controls should then be established over the actual delivery of merchandise and payment by the customer to the issuing cashier, and over the accounting follow-up of the transaction and transfer of funds.

Cash receipts should not be used directly to pay expenses. The cashier must bank the funds collected without applying them to the payment of expenses.

Finally, a person from the accounting department will compare the total of the invoices with the amounts received by the cashier or with the notice from the bank (daily tally). Any discrepancy must be immediately checked and possibly reported directly to a responsible person.

c) Financial costs of treasury operations

These charges must be checked to ensure that they comply with the rates and scales agreed upon with the bank beforehand. The priority is to control the agios and commissions charged.

C) Retention of cash values

i. Retention of checks

Checks not yet used should be kept in a safe place under the responsibility of one person. Used and completed checkbooks should be archived and filed for retention as evidence of payment.

ii. Check and Cash Deposit

The monitoring of the company's cash flow is not only related to the monitoring of the payment and remittance of checks to the payment. It is necessary to check the accounting entries through samples and to verify, for a certain number of transactions, the remittance slips, the credit notes, and the corresponding statements. Also, it is necessary to permanently check the value dates and verify the agios calculations.

On another level of analysis, cash and checks should be deposited in the bank quickly. The main purpose of this operation is to limit the amounts available to the treasury and consequently limit the related risks of loss or fraud.

Finally, the control of treasury operations implies that the persons who guarantee the deposit of cheques in the bank and the recording of transactions in the company's accounts are independent.

iii. Safeguarding of cash assets

The assets should be safeguarded and kept in a safe place (safe) under the responsibility of a limited number of people in the management. The person in charge of the fund should not have access to other funds. In addition, he/she should not be involved in approving or authorizing settlement vouchers.

D) Accounting of transactions in connection with the treasury

i. Segregation of duties

The accounting journals in connection with the treasury must be established by a person who does not have access to the "customer" or "supplier" accounts. Also, the writing and signing of checks must be entrusted to a person who has no relationship with the accounting recording of accounts.

The company must provide additional controls even if this principle is followed, since it does not allow for exhaustive control, especially in cases where it is impossible to separate these functions. Also, the person responsible for the accounting records should not establish the bank reconciliation to control the bank accounts.

ii. Monitoring of records

The use of a specific journal for each of the currencies is important for the control of records, especially when evaluating exchange rates. Checks should be recorded as soon as they are issued and money received as soon as it is received. This recording mechanism avoids any oversight or delay. The recording of issued checks should be done in a numerical sequence. It is also possible to verify that all checks have been recorded by checking the cash journals against the checkbook stubs.

iii. Bank Reconciliation

Bank balances regularly require reconciliation of the amounts on the bank statements with those in the accounting records. The objective is to detect any errors that may have been made by the bank or by the company's accountant. The bank reconciliation consists in comparing the accounting records of the bank account with the transactions appearing on the bank statement. It allows following the cash flow of the company is to make decisions and manage customer reminders and the supplier payments.

Generally, there are several discrepancies between these two documents, as well as several errors or omissions:
- accounting errors (e.g.: reversals of figures, transactions recorded twice, entries recorded in the "wrong" bank account, etc.)
- anomalies due to the banker (recording errors, amount errors, etc.)
- The bank reconciliation is necessary because there are discrepancies between: the date of registration of an incoming or outgoing payment on the bank statement and the date on which it is appropriate to proceed with the registration of an incoming or outgoing payment.
  - errors when entering amounts
  - omissions in the entry of bank charges, agios, etc.
  - cash receipts not yet recorded, checks not debited, etc.
  - withdrawals made by the bank of which the company was not aware.

A bank reconciliation is not mandatory, but it can be very useful. It is advisable to perform it at least once a month. The optimal frequency depends on the number and importance of the operations carried out.

E) The internal audit approach of the treasury department

The existence of internal control allows the auditor to assess the effectiveness of internal control, mainly through compliance and permanence tests. Therefore, the audit of the treasury cycle mainly concerns:

- The overall completeness of records;
- Examination of the control systems (compliance tests)
- Examination of the control systems (permanence tests)
- Specific examinations related to misappropriation techniques.

1) Overall completeness of accounting records

The internal auditor must ensure that all payments and receipts are recorded. The audit focuses on the detection of recording errors or omissions.

2) Examination of the control systems

The auditor aims to monitor representative operations by ensuring that the documents, classifications, and controls correspond to the structural reality of the organization according to the nomenclature presented in the procedures manual.

The expenditure and payment procedure:

This procedure requires a thorough control of:
- The preservation of checkbooks and cash balances;
- The establishment of crossed checks only;
- The existence of supporting documents signed by an official for any payment;
- Limitation of persons authorizing payments. These persons must be experienced and in contact with the cashier or the person signing the checks;
- The existence of a procedure for exceptional payments;

- Issuance of checks in digital sequence.

Control of cash accounting transactions:

The control of accounting transactions primarily addresses the following:
- Pre-numbering of supporting documents;
- Detailed arithmetic control of entries based on supporting documents;
- Periodic supervision of the different cash journals by an independent person;
- Reconciliation with bank statements and accounts.
- Reciprocal control between the different treasury accounts;
- Monthly bank reconciliation with the bank accounts;
- Inventory of the cash.

Monitoring of accounts and physical protection of assets

- A great speed of the handing-over in cash;
- Optimal frequency of bank transfers;
- Protection of assets within the company (safe, access codes, etc.).

3) Periodic monitoring of control systems
The objective of this ongoing test is to ensure that the advantages of the internal control process identified during previous audit missions are still operational.

> ➢ **For payments**

- Verify records on the bank statement and look for the record in the accounting system;
- Review bank reconciliations and verify payments that appear in the reconciliation;
- Test the records from the checkbooks or some checkbooks (large amounts, specific amounts ... etc.);
- Validate that canceled checks cannot be reused;
- Checks issued against bank statements;
- Bring back checks from the bank and examine whether the payee matches the records made by the company;

- Analyze outstanding checks in detail;
- Collect payment dates on checks and compare them with issue dates and accounting dates;
- Monitor inter-bank transfers.

> ### For revenue

- Ensure that receipts are recorded in the accounts by comparing them with the bank statement;
- Verify the recording of extra-accounting records of receipts in the accounts;
- Systematically check receipts and remittances, noting any discrepancies between deposits and recordings by the bank. If necessary, ask the bank for copies of the remittance slips (to check for discrepancies);
- Checking discounts given to customers to ensure that they have not been marked up.
- Checking totals in revenue records;
- Systematic tallying of recorded receipts with supporting documents.

> ### The reality of the records

The main issue here is to check whether all records are authorized and correspond to the operation and interest of the company or whether there are records of unauthorized payments. There are therefore two aspects to this risk:
- Either the payments are made without authorization or are payments that have already been made, with the associated risk of double payment;
- Or it is a question of fictitious payments that result in a misappropriation of funds.

Following this diagnosis, the internal auditor softens or consolidates his intervention and account control program. Also, he must ensure the validity of the accounting charges for each item on the balance sheet. The objective of this verification is to make an objective assessment of the quality and relevance of the summary statements.

After an analysis of all these elements, the internal auditor formulates an opinion on the company's situation. He must present his opinion on the fairness, regularity, and true and fair view of the summary statements. However, other control mechanisms are necessary given specific cases of embezzlement or fraud.

4) Specific examinations related to detour techniques

a) Possible embezzlement techniques
There are two main possibilities for embezzlement of funds, either of receipts or sums available in cash or in the bank.

1) Embezzlement of revenues
To detect and identify such misappropriations, the internal auditor may use several audit methods. The main misappropriation techniques are:
- Leaving accounts receivable in debit even after payment;
- Writing off "receivables" accounts with losses;
- Failure to record revenue;
- Recording fictitious assets;
- Manipulating bank reconciliations;
- Cascading and linking records to conceal the initial misappropriation.

2) Misappropriation of cash or bank balances
Several manipulations can be used to divert assets such as

- Raising the total of payments;
- Not accounting for suppliers' assets;
- Adding fictitious headcount;
- Create fictitious expense vouchers;
- Reusing vouchers.

b) Special procedures and reviews

1) Bank reconciliation

This reconciliation is for:
- A review of bank statements;
- Performing bank reconciliations and comparing them to the

Internal Audit of Treasury and cash management

company's statements.

2) Final consistency check

This final step mainly consists of a quick change of all the different accounts and cash journals.

Once completed, the internal auditor begins a global recapitulation of all the operations examined. For this reason, he may draw up summary and recapitulation tables with and final reports. The objective of these documents is to serve as best as possible to rectify the errors detected.

F) Internal audit tools for the cash cycle

The internal auditor uses several tools at his disposal to carry out his missions. The mastery of the use of these tools helps him to reach his objectives with greater speed and efficiency. We will present the main tools that can be used by the internal auditor:
- Information gathering instruments
- Descriptive methods
- Diagnostic tools
- Validation techniques

1. Information gathering instruments

Information collection tools are generally the most widely used. We distinguish:

o **The audit interview**
This is the most preliminary aspect of the audit and consists of questioning the participants on specific questions related to the internal audit mission. This tool is difficult to conduct given the methodological constraints of qualitative studies and therefore requires advance preparation.

o **Direct observation**
Physical observation by the auditor is an application tool, as all managerial phenomena are observable. An audit mission cannot be limited to interviews, because it could be considered as an opinion poll. Indeed, the interview is far from being sufficient to understand

the procedures.

Two approaches to observation are generally classified: quantitative observation of assets and qualitative observation. We also distinguish:

- Document observation
- Behavioral observation: The direct observation of behaviors is the one that allows the direct observation of the studied phenomenon. Indirect observation of behavior involves a third party who will examine on behalf of the auditor and will entrust him with the result of his observation.

The auditor who observes often raises issues that are more confidential and hidden and cannot be deduced from the analysis of written documents. Observation is a rich source of distinctive examples that are useful in illustrating the conclusions reached by the internal auditor.

o   **The questionnaire**

There are often typical, standardized questionnaires for internal auditing assignments. A distinction is made between:
- Open or closed-ended questionnaire
- Multiple choice questionnaire
- Internal control questionnaire (ICQ)

The auditor must adapt the tool used to the audited company and the sector.

o   **Statistical surveys**

This is a method which allows, based on a random sample, in a reference population, to extrapolate to the population, the observations made on the sample. The survey as an audit technique consists of taking a sample from a population of individuals, examining it in detail, and drawing a conclusion about the whole population from this control.

2.   Descriptive methods

There are normally four main instruments for descriptive methods:

o   **Flowcharts**

Flowcharts can be collected or designed by the internal auditor as needed. The auditor is often faced with obsolete flowcharts and therefore has to update or adapt them to his needs. Today, there are specialized software programs oriented toward the rapid and adapted drawing of various organizational charts.

o **The narrative**

Narratives are information and documents designed by the auditor in which he explains how the procedures are carried out within the audited company. The main objective of narratives is to allow the auditor to have a clear representation of the procedures and processes within the audited entity. This technique consists of describing the procedure in force in the form of a written document that summarizes all the information gathered on the procedure under study.

The advantage of the narrative is that it can be done by the auditor whatever his mastery of the process. Also, the narrative creates a good working climate between the auditor and the audited. Finally, the narration allows having a richness of information obtained.

However, in the process of narration it is generally difficult to find the information sought in the partner's speech (Lamsiah et al., 2021). Indeed, generally, the speech can be abused and the parentheses and detours often drown out the essence of the speech. Also, there are cases where it is difficult to understand what is meant through these phrases or the technical terms, abbreviations, and other locutions used.

o **The diagrams**

The diagram is a description formalizing a movement of information. It is a tool used to develop an understanding of a process. Generally, firms and researchers have developed standardized symbols for drawing these diagrams.

It is an aid to the:
- Visualization
- Synthesis and conciseness
- Accuracy

Some rules must be followed for diagrams:
- Use one diagram per procedure;
- Divide the diagrams in case of a complex procedure;
- Respect the chronology of operations;
- Put the source of the documents;
- Use a comment column to explain the diagram;

It must allow us to visualize:
- The type of document,
- The number of copies,
- The origin of the document,
- The destination,
- Its filing method,
- The controls carried out.

The auditor should put on file a copy of each of the documents mentioned in the detailed diagram.

o **Separation of duties grids**

It allows to display the different tasks performed for each procedure and checks the cases of incompatibility and overlapping of tasks. It is a snapshot of the work distribution at a given time. It is a statistical document that allows us to identify the failures in the separation of tasks and to bring remedies. The segregation of duties chart is used to justify the choice of positions and to analyze workloads. It allows for the identification of segregation of duties violations.

o **The Problem Analysis and Revelation Sheet**

This is a summary document that allows you to summarize the nature of the problems, the risk, assess the cause, then the consequences, and to propose recommendations.

3. The tools of knowledge and diagnosis

The techniques used are the following:
- Information analysis;
- Search for convincing indicators;
- Use of financial analysis ratios;
- Analytical review;
- Reasonableness check.

They are used to assess control and control risk.

4. Validation techniques

o **Arithmetic and valuation checks**

These checks consist of verifying additions, multiplications and also transfers. It is a question of making estimates on the evaluation methods and calculations of costs, depreciation and provisions, etc., without recalculating everything.

o **Document control**

This is a technique that consists of extracting and processing existing information on the company's paper or electronic media.
The auditor must look for evidence to validate the balances of the accounts. He must give more value to the documents coming from third parties. Document control also includes sequence checks, transcription and reconciliation.

o **Third Party Confirmation**

One of the most valuable techniques is direct third party confirmation.

The main third parties involved are:
- Suppliers
- Customers
- Banks

Confirmation requests with third parties can be closed or open. Confirmation requests to customers are generally closed, those to suppliers, and banks are more often open.

o **Computerized tools**

Today, many tools are computerized. Therefore, most auditors or internal audit departments create their own IT tools.

The management of financial and monetary flows in companies and other organizational forms is reserved for the treasury function. It encompasses two main components, namely liquidity management and financial risk management (Hubert, 1997).

Internal Audit of Treasury and cash management

Internal Audit of Treasury and cash management

Part Two:
Internal Audit of the Treasury Cycle: Practical Aspects

CHAPTER 1

METHODOLOGY, OBJECTIVES AND DETAILED APPROACH OF THE CASH CYCLE AUDIT

The methodology is the set of techniques and methods used to guide the development of research. The objective is to guide the scientific process. The methodology allows not only to carry out the investigations, but also for the readers to follow with ease the explained sequence. Research in management sciences and in particular in internal auditing uses a wide variety of methodological approaches. The use of a research method is the normal consequence of a methodological and epistemological choice.

Objectivism considers that the researcher has the position of an external observer. In other words, one observes without acting. In a positivist/rationalist position, the world is external to the individual. One insists on observable facts to validate the approach or the theoretical reasoning developed. Thus, truth is looked at from an objective point of view as a product of pure reason. Subjectivism, on the other hand, considers the opposite, i.e. that the researcher is in the position of an active participant. Interpretive theories sought to go beyond a research framework strongly impregnated with structural-functionalist theories by focusing attention on the interpretive patterns of individuals. According to them, management practices are constructed by social actors and, consequently, can be modified by them.

From a constructivist or phenomenological/existential perspective, the world is seen as a social construct and as the product of intuitions determined by individuals. For this school of thought, there is no effective criterion of scientific truth. Thus, research is defined through the action and interventions of actors through their cognitive processes.

The conception of knowledge proposed by constructivist epistemologies is a conception characterized by the hypothesis of cognitive feasibility. This non-Cartesian epistemology challenges the methodological primacy of reductionism in the development of knowledge. With such an epistemological position, management research focuses its attention on the explanation of phenomena and not on their prediction. According to the constructivist paradigm, there is not one reality that can be apprehended, even in an imperfect manner, but multiple realities that are the product of individual or collective mental constructions and that are likely to evolve over time.

The data for our practical sheets on the internal audit of the cash cycle will be collected through individual interviews and direct observation. These two methods are possible given that we have practiced internal auditing within several companies and also that we have proceeded by analyzing documents and management situations in their real contexts to understand the emergence and evolution of certain phenomena. The method that will be used is therefore qualitative given the relationship of the subject with a framework of qualitative data. These data provide enriched, in-depth, and diversified information. They are based on individuals or a few cases. Therefore, our approach will be based on the study of possible cases and completed by complementary confirmatory case studies.

Among the tasks of the internal auditor, we can mention:
- Permanent control of procedures
- Surprise control of cash in hand
- Control of bank reconciliations
- Request for confirmation of bank balances
- Control of signatures on checks

Like any audit, the cash cycle audit requires a specific approach, tools, and objectives. According to Becours and Bouquin (2008), there are five general steps for the audit of the cash cycle in a company:
- Review of goals
- Review of objectives
- Review of means

- Review of internal organization
- Overall evaluation of the treasury in terms of effectiveness, efficiency, economy, security, and relevance.

Our analysis approach will be based on the following model (Figure 2):

o Analysis and diagnosis of the existing situation: Review of the existing situation and collection of information,
o Detailed control on the documents and with the help of interviews using audit models of the cash cycle,
o Recommendations, anomaly detection, and action plan,
o Implementation of the action plan through corrective measures and prospects.

We have summarized our approach in the following diagram (Figure 2):

Figure 2: Internal Audit Approach

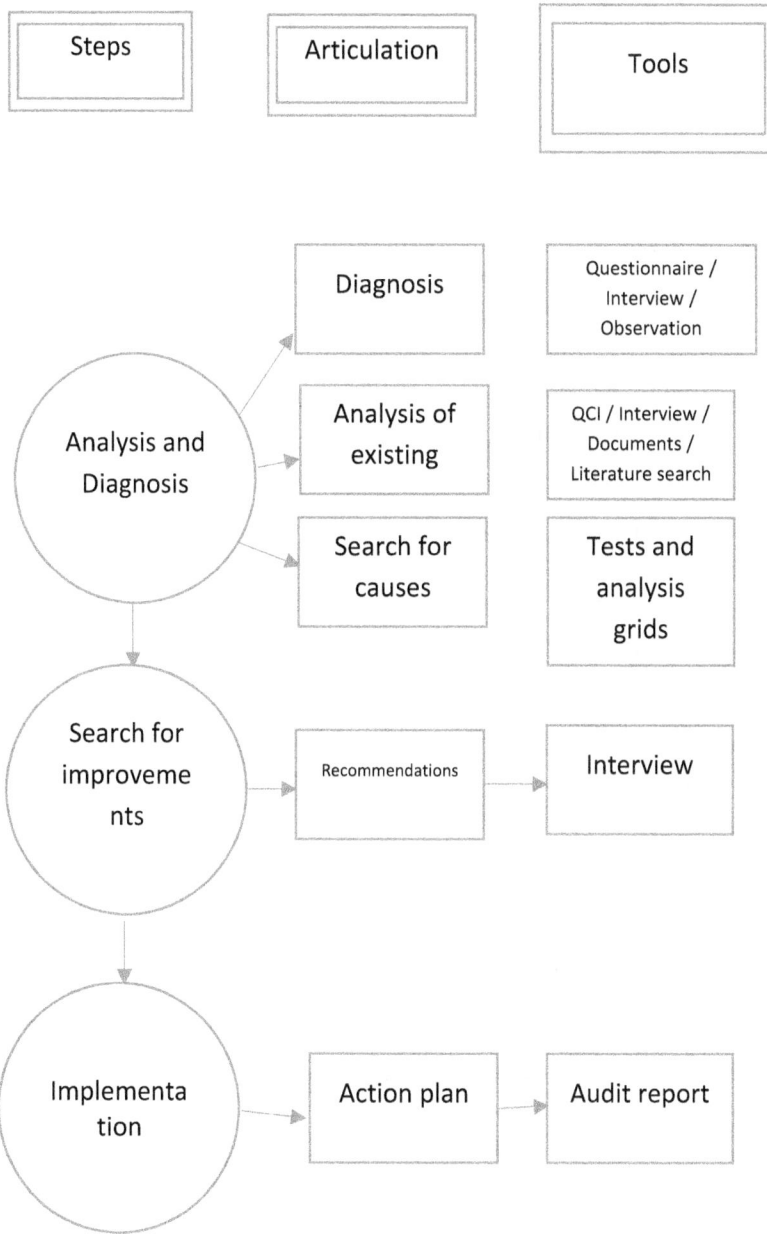

The evaluation of the internal control system related to the cash cycle was carried out at the end of this stage about the main evaluation techniques. For this reason, we have detailed our audit documents used by dividing them into three categories according to the following plan:

A) Preliminary audit phase
A-1: Knowledge of the entity and its environment
A-2: Description of the tasks
A-3: Diagnosis of procedures
A-4: Risk analysis and risk register.
A-5: Materiality threshold.
A-6: Audit strategy plan and approach.

B) Detailed audit phase
B-1: Separation of duties grid.
B-2: Internal control questionnaire.
B-3: Detailed plan of the treasury audit.
B-4: Compliance tests on the expenditure system (national, international, and by fund).
B-5: Continuity test on the preparation of bank reconciliation statements.
B-6: Control of bank account documents.
B-7: Confirmation of the third party.
B-8: The payment dashboard
B-9: Cash flow reporting
B-10: Bank commission follow-up sheet
B-11: Currency conversion sheet
B-12: Discount follow-up

C) Synthesis and completion phase
C-1: Summary of Major Findings
C-2: Audit completion review.

CHAPTER 2

A PRACTICAL APPROACH TO THE INTERNAL AUDIT OF THE CASH CYCLE

A/ The preliminary phase of the audit

As part of the process of understanding the characteristics of the company's operations, the internal auditor aims to gather information on the following areas:
- General Information;
- Technical characteristics of the company;
- Commercial characteristics of the company;
- Legal characteristics of the company.

Acceptance of the treasury's internal audit assignment must be evidenced by the signing of an engagement letter that will constitute the contract describing the rights and duties of each of the contracting parties. This engagement letter must contain:

1. Identification of the parties,
2. The work to be done and the objective of the mission,
3. The duration of the mission
4. The resources to be made available to the auditor
5. The general conditions of the intervention (conduct of the mission),
6. The respective obligations of the parties,
7. The procedure to follow in case of a dispute.

Thus, the engagement letter sets a framework for the relationship between the two parties by establishing rights and obligations for each of them. Its objective is to guarantee the smooth running of the mission.

A-1) Knowledge of the entity and its environment

The auditor must gather information on the reasons for the creation of the company, its commercial development, and information on the legal aspects. Thus, the analysis of the history of the company's development can help the auditor to understand its current situation and often allows to situate it in its environment.

Obtaining the organization chart at this stage of the mission seems essential since it will allow the auditor to understand the organization of the company and identify the main responsibilities. It will also be useful during the course of the engagement, to identify the persons to be contacted during the course of the internal audit engagement.

The auditor should gather all information related to the organization of the accounting and finance departments, the systems or software in use, the various controls in place, and the internal procedures. The auditor should obtain a copy of the organization and accounting procedures manual. If no such manual exists, the internal auditor should schedule interviews with key managers to identify the procedures in place within the company.

The internal auditor of the treasury cycle takes note of:

- The entity's industry, its regulatory environment, including the applicable financial reporting framework, and other external factors such as general economic conditions;
- The characteristics of the entity that enable the auditor to understand the types of transactions, account balances, and disclosures expected in the notes to the financial statements. These characteristics include in particular the nature of its activities, the composition of its capital and corporate governance, its investment policy, its organization, and financing, as well as the choice of accounting methods applied;
- The entity's objectives and the strategies implemented to achieve them insofar as these objectives may have financial consequences and, therefore, an impact on the accounts;
- The measurement and analysis of the entity's financial performance

indicators; these elements indicate to the auditor the financial aspects that management considers to be of major concern;
- Internal control elements relevant to the audit.

In this step, the aim is to discover the audited company and its characteristics. The proposed model is set out in Form A-1: Knowledge of the entity and its environment. This examination can be completed by Form A-1': Report of discussions/interviews with the audit team.

Internal Audit of Treasury and cash management

Form A-1: Knowledge of the entity and its environment

"Company name"	Year:.........
A-1	Knowledge of the entity and its environment

OBJECTIVE
The objective is to obtain and document knowledge about the entity and its environment to provide a basis for identifying and assessing the risks of material misstatement.

Basic information	Comments	Significant risks
History		
Date of incorporation		
Change of activities		
Markets		
Significant acquisition		
Disposal		
Sector Overview		
General economic conditions		
Technological change		
Likely future developments		
Legal or regulatory changes		
competitive factors		
Strategy		
Current objectives and strategies		
Origins of competitive advantages/plans to maintain or develop them		
Shareholders, directors and employees		
Parties with the control authority		
Managers and roles		
Staff member		
Internal Audit		
Existence of an internal audit function		
Products and processes		
The products		

Market		
Suppliers Customers Competitors		
Property, plant and equipment		
Significant information about fixed assets		
Cash-flow and financing		
How the entity is structured and how it is financed? important points about recevables, payables, inventories, and leases.		
Taxes on sales transactions		
Applicable tax regime		
Accounting rules		
Accounting rules		
Laws and regulations		
Acquire a general knowledge of the applicable legal and regulatory framework		
Environmental issues		
Customer attitude/internal policy toward environmental aspects Published policies/statements, external perception		
Governance Issues		
How many directors sit on the board of directors? How long can a director serve on the board? What is the process for appointing new directors? Does the board have a charter? Are the policies (e.g., code of conduct) of the board and the entity documented?		

Form A-1': Report of discussions/interviews with the audit team

"Company name"	Year:.........
A-1'	Report of discussions/interviews with the audit team

OBJECTIVE
The purpose of this checklist is to document the discussions that took place within the audit team. Communication among the audit team members is necessary for all phases of the engagement to ensure that all issues have been appropriately addressed.

Areas of discussion	Comments
Data from the previous audit (nature of the entity, internal control, type of audit opinion, significant risks, specific issues, etc.)	
Significant risks	
Responses to risks	
Continuity of operations	
Risk of fraud	
Changes (new activity, new regulations, new management, etc.)	
Specific resources (expert, specialized auditor, etc.)	
Definition of the roles of the members of the audit team: Engagement partner Quality control manager Other	

A-2) Description of the tasks

The accounting department performs several tasks related to the cash cycle by several actors:

- **The Chief Accountant**

The chief accountant is the primary person responsible for cash management. He is responsible for:
- Ensure the supervision and monitoring of the cash flow;
- Ensure relations with banks;
- Negotiate, harmonize and ensure the strict application of banking conditions;
- Manage treasury operations initiated by his/her departments.

- **The treasurer for national payments**

The Corporate Treasurer for Domestic Payments reports directly to the Chief Financial Officer. Duties include:
- Analyze bank statements;
- Prepare payment orders and checks;
- Monitor bank balances, account balancing, and short-term investments;
- Negotiate foreign exchange rates with the trading room;
- Ensure the updating of cash flow forecasts;
- Monitor and prepare disbursements;
- Establish the cash flow statement and monthly reporting.

- **The treasurer for international payments**

He/she reports to the Administrative and Financial Director. His/her tasks are:
- Analyze bank statements;
- Prepare payment orders;
- Monitor bank balances;
- Negotiate exchange rates with the trading room;
- Follow up on the setting up and monitoring of guarantees;
- Provide forecasts based on expenditure commitments;
- Provide forecasts based on expenditure commitments; Ensure the

updating of cash flow forecasts;
- Monitor and prepare disbursements;
- Establish the cash-flow statement and monthly reporting.

- **Department Accountant:**

His tasks are:
- Ensure that forecasts are entered with the corresponding budget elements;
- Improve the regular processing time of accounting documents;
- Analyze suspense items (bank error, data entry error, incomplete setup) and follow up on placements;
- Receive commercial service invoices;
- Ensure the accounting of payments.

The internal auditor must adapt the treasurers' assignments to the entities being audited. Indeed, there is a great divergence in these missions between entities of different sizes or activities.

A-3) Diagnosis of procedures

In this section, we will present the different payment procedures that can be considered. There are three main procedures: payment of local suppliers, payment of foreign suppliers, and payment by the cashier.

Internal Audit of Treasury and cash management

1) Payment of national suppliers

Table 5: Payment procedure for domestic suppliers

Step	Intervener	Description	Documents
1	Department concerned	Manifestation of a need for a material or service	Work Flow Cost Center in the IT system
2	Purchasing Department	Establishment of a purchase order	Purchase order based on the purchase request
3	Purchasing Department	Validation of the purchase order, quotation, and approval of the order by a double signature	Approval of the purchase order by the Purchasing Manager and the Financial Director.
4	Storekeeper	Receipt of goods	Delivery order
5	Sales department	Control of the quantities purchased Rejection of non-conforming materials	Invoice
6	Accounting department	Receipt of invoices	Invoice purchase order delivery order
7	Treasurer	Receipt of the file	Payment order or check
8	Accounting department	Control of the parts and acknowledgment of receipt	Accounting software
9	Treasurer	Preparation of the payment and control of the documents	Accounting file
10	Treasurer	Entering the accounting operation	Payment reconciliation.

Internal Audit of Treasury and cash management

Figure 3: Document flow diagram for the national payments procedure

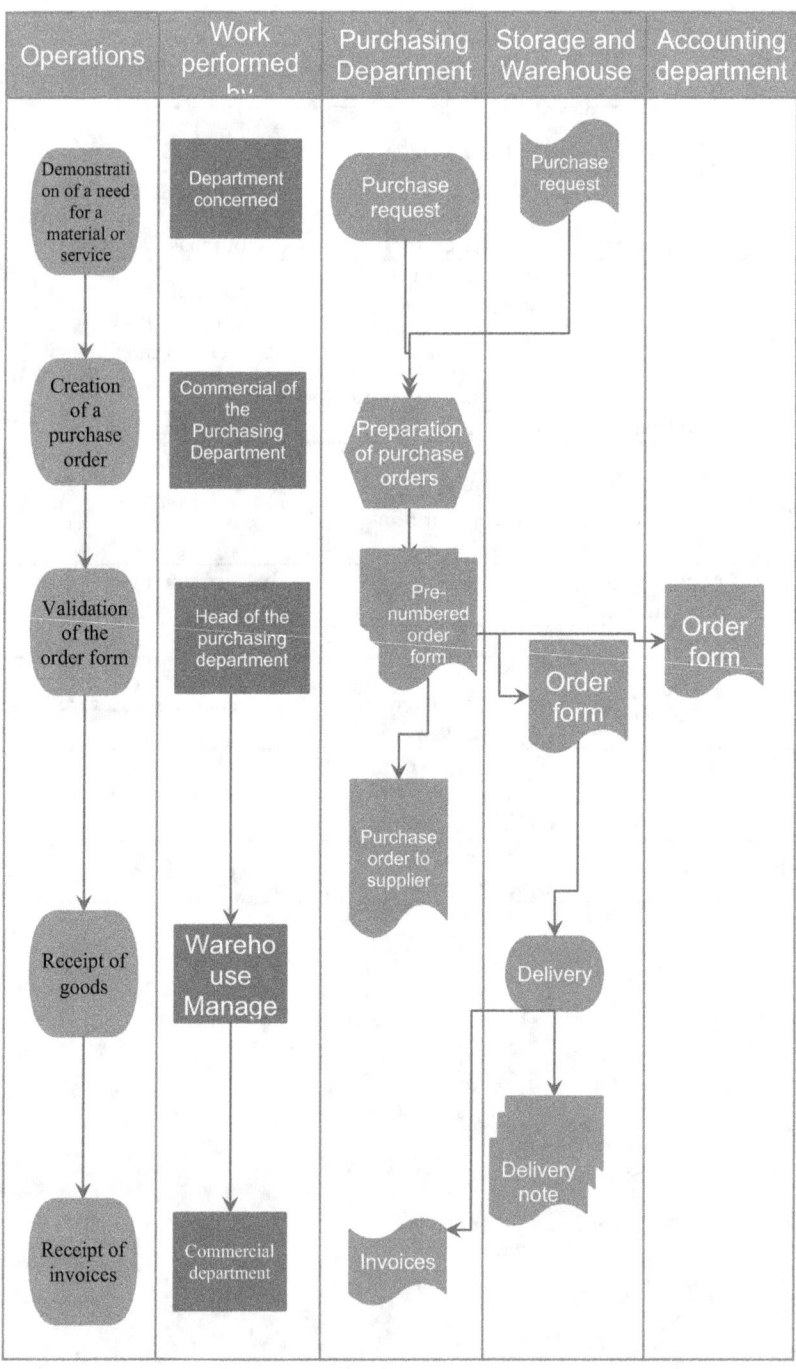

Internal Audit of Treasury and cash management

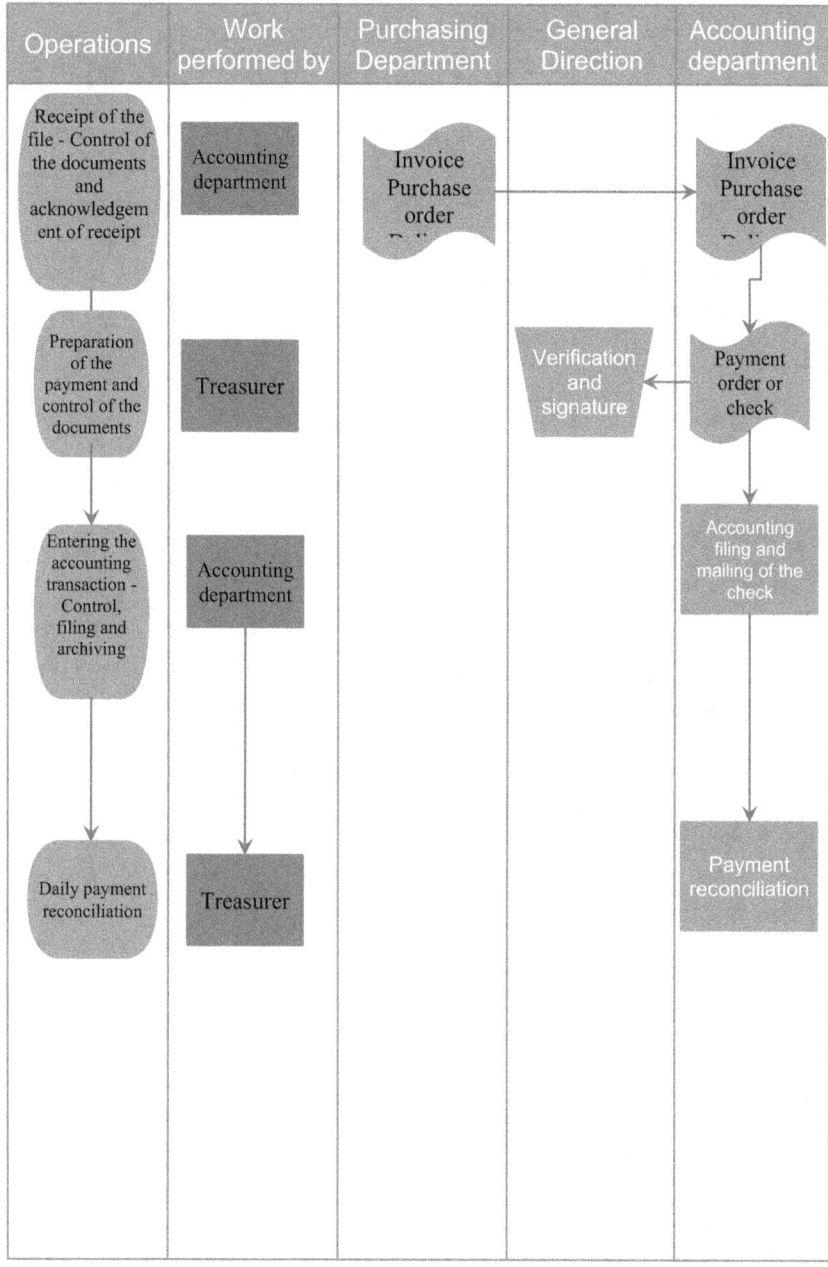

Internal Audit of Treasury and cash management

2) Payment of international suppliers

Table 6: Payment procedure for international suppliers

Step	Intervener	Description	Documents
1	Department concerned	Manifestation of an internal material need	Stock requirement form with material nomenclature
2	Commercial department	Choice of the supplier	Choice by several predefined criteria
3	Commercial department	Placement of the order	Order
4	Commercial department	Logistic follow-up of the material	Digital platform
5	Import-Export	Domiciliation of the import notice	Import commitment and direct debit (Company, bank, and forwarder)
6	Freight forwarder	Physical clearance	Digital platform
7	Freight forwarder	Validation of customs clearance	Import declaration and registration number
8	Warehouseman	Reception of materials	Packaging list and quantity tally
9	Storekeeper	Quality control by the material quality laboratory	Material control form
10	Commercial service	Verification of the purchase order	Invoice Purchase order and delivery note
11	Treasurer	Preparation of the payment	Import commitment, Invoice and packaging list, and bank transfer order
12	Accounting department	Entering of the third party and lettering	Accounting journal
13	Treasurer	Execution of payment	Sending of documents
14	Accounting department	Entry of payments in the journal	Accounting journal
15	Accounting department	Filing and archiving	Accounting archives

3) Cash payment

Table 7: Payment procedure by Caisse

Step	Intervener	Description	Documents
1	Department concerned	Manifestation of a need	Request for payment
2	Cashier	Payment	Order for payment in cash.

A-4) Risk analysis and risk register

The main roles of internal audit in the risk management process are to (IAA, 2004):
- Assure risk management processes.
- Assure that risks are properly assessed.
- Evaluate risk management processes.
- Evaluate the communication of major risks.
- Review the management of major risks.

The risk analysis consists of three complementary phases:
o Risk identification;
o Definition and delimitation of risks;
o Risk assessment.

The identification, analysis, and prioritization of risks allow us to define the preventive actions to be implemented, covering the technical, human, and organizational dimensions.

We have identified and prioritized the various risks associated with the cash cycle. For this purpose, we have used Form A-4: Risk analysis and risk register. This form can be completed or adapted according to the different risks by using the risk table presented.

"Company name"		Year: ....
A-4	**ANALYSIS OF THE RISK OF MATERIAL MISSTATEMENT** Purchasing/supplier cycle	

Form A-4: Risk analysis and risk register

OBJECTIVE
The purpose of this checklist is to document the assessment of the combined risks of material misstatement at the assertion level of the purchasing/supplier cycle. This assessment will serve as a basis for determining the nature, extent, and timing of further audit procedures to be performed that address the identified risks.

1. INHERENT RISKS		
Question	YES/NO	Comments
Are the suppliers' payment terms normal?		
Is the company dependent on one or more suppliers?		
Is the company's purchasing policy organized?		
Are suppliers diligent in issuing their invoices quickly?		

2. CONTROL RISKS		
Question	YES/NO	Comments
Is there an authorization process for orders?		
Are there pre-numbered receipt slips?		
Are the quality and quantity controls of the receipts subject to a visa materialized by an independent person?		
When invoices are received, is there an **ORIGINAL** stamp or official signature on one of the copies received?		
Are invoices reconciled with receipt slips and purchase orders?		
Do the invoices include the accounting charge?		
Do they include a payment reference?		
Is there a visa for entry and payment?		
Is the supplier's accounting up to date?		
Are payments made systematically based on a supporting document?		

Cycle purchases/suppliers		Risk (Y/N)	Risk level (H, M, L) H: High, M: Medium, L: Low	Comments
3. CONCLUSIONS				
Inherent risks	Double payment of the same invoice			
	Loss of discounts			
	Late payment			
Control risks	The same number of accounting documents			
	Assignment of the same registration number			
	Absence of supporting documents			

Internal Audit of Treasury and cash management

	"Company name"	Year: ....
A-4	ANALYSES OF THE RISKS OF MATERIAL MISSTATEMENT	
	Annual financial statements are taken as a whole	

OBJECTIVE

The objective is to assess the combined risks of material misstatement of the financial statements.

It will serve as a basis for determining the nature and extent of further audit procedures to be performed to address the risks identified.

1. INHERENT RISKS

1.1. ORGANIZATION - MANAGEMENT

Question	YES/NO	Comments
Is management attentive to the auditor's work?		
Does management have the appropriate knowledge and experience to properly prepare the entity's financial statements?		
Is the quality of the financial information produced by management in previous years satisfactory?		
Does the organization and management of the company allow avoiding important disputes (customers, suppliers, personnel, products, etc.)?		
Is the accounting management stable?		
Are the relations with the personnel good?		

1.2. PREPARATION OF ANNUAL ACCOUNTS

Question	YES/NO	Comments
Have previous audits revealed a few anomalies in the accounting and financial information?		
Does the nature of the company's operations generate simple accounting entries?		
Does the company make frequent changes in valuation methods?		
If there is a cost accounting system, are its data consistent with those of the general accounting system?		

1.3. LINE OF BUSINESS

Question	YES/NO	Comments
Is the evolution of the market in which the company is located favorable?		
Is the company's activity linked to innovations or technological changes?		
According to the study of the financial structure and profitability ratios (sectoral references), is the company developing by its sector?		
If the company is expanding rapidly, are the consequences on the necessary resources under control?		
Are the company's supplies and outlets stable (absence of loss of an important customer or supplier)?		
Is a restructuring/reorganization operation underway or planned?		

1.4. LEGAL AND REGULATORY ENVIRONMENT		
Question	YES /NO	Comments
Is management sufficiently aware of the legal and regulatory texts?		
Is a major legal transaction underway or planned?		

2. CONTROL RISKS

2.1. CONTROL ENVIRONMENT		
Question	YES /NO	Comments
Do managers and executives demonstrate integrity in their behavior?		
Does management seek to comply with legal and regulatory requirements, including tax and labor regulations?		
Does management demonstrate an interest in the quality of internal control and administrative procedures?		
Does it periodically ensure this quality?		
Is management aware of the importance of accounting controls?		
Has it given sufficient attention to our previous recommendations?		
Does management have an interest in the quality of accounting and financial reporting?		
Are the accounts kept up to date?		
If there is a procedure manual, is it regularly updated?		

Internal Audit of Treasury and cash management

2.2. MEANS OF IDENTIFYING RISKS RELATED TO THE ACTIVITY		
Question	YES/NO	Comments
Is the manager involved in the company's activity?		
Does the manager pay sufficient attention to the risks inherent in the business?		
Does the accounting staff have the appropriate training?		
Does the manager have steering tools?		
Does the company have sufficient information on accounting, tax, and social matters?		
2.3. INFORMATION SYSTEMS		
Question	YES/NO	Comments
Does management have control over the IT function?		
Was it possible to obtain a description of the types of software and applications?		
Is it standard software?		
Is the software used to process accounting and financial information reliable?		
Has the manager developed and implemented an appropriate information systems contingency plan to ensure the continued operation of the business in the event of a disaster?		
Has the manager developed and implemented appropriate transaction authorization procedures, including procedures to prevent unauthorized changes to data files and programs?		
Is the computer system sustainable?		
Is the computer system adequate to handle the entity's operations?		

3. SUMMARY OF GENERAL INHERENT RISK				
Topics	Risk level (H, M, L) H: High, M: Medium, L: Low			Comments
	H	M	L	
3.1. ORGANIZATION - MANAGEMENT				
3.2. PREPARATION OF ACCOUNTS				
3.3. BUSINESS SEGMENT				
3.4. LEGAL AND REGULATORY ENVIRONMENT				
4. SUMMARY OF CONTROL RISKS				
Topics	Risk level (H, M, L) H: High, M: Medium, L: Low			Comments
	H	M	L	
4.1. CONTROL ENVIRONMENT				
4.2. MEANS OF IDENTIFYING RISKS RELATED TO THE ACTIVITY				
4.3. INFORMATION SYNTHESIS				

Internal Audit of Treasury and cash management

"Company name"	Year : ....
A-4	**CASH CYCLE ISK REGISTER**

OBJECTIVE

The objective is to document and list the treasury cycle risks identified during the treasury procedures with the probability of occurrence and the impact (based on a scale of 1 to 5) of the potential error in the financial statements (at the assertion level) resulting from the risks and to discuss the risk register with management to validate the completeness and relevance of the assessment.

Risk No.	Description of the risk	What error can result from this?	Risk analysis			
			Probability of occurrence (1-5) (a)	Impact (1-5) (b)	Combined risk (a) x (b)	Significant risk (Y/N) ?
1	Misappropriation through manipulation of accounts	Loss of value				
2	Error or omission in recording repatriations	Error in the evaluation of exchange rates				
3	Presence of unjustified cash vouchers	Fraudulent payments				
4	Current accounts in deficit	Domestic or international payments without estimates				
5	Non-exhaustiveness of records	Double registration or non-payment to suppliers				
6	Risk of certification reservation by the auditor	Errors in recording or estimating				
7	Falsification of third party accounts	Third-party				
8	Error in the estimation of the exchange rate to be used for the accounting of payments	Error in the estimation of exchange rate differences				
9	Uncontrolled increase in financial expenses	Excessive bank commissions				
10	Non-balancing of bank accounts	Bank debit balance				
	(.....)					

Internal Audit of Treasury and cash management

Internal Audit of Treasury and cash management

Examples of Fraud and possible risks	Significant risk (Y/N)?
Expenses allocated too early or too late and other manipulations affecting asset accounts	
Inconsistency and/or changes in valuation rules	
Capitalization of costs (internal costing), restructuring costs, development costs, and other services and goods	
Revaluation of assets	
Sale of assets at an inflated price, which may indicate injection of funds for laundering	
False down payments on assets under construction	
Purchase of shares at inflated prices	
Valuation of participations	
Accounting for equity investments: cash investments	
Exaggeration regarding the quality of inventories	
The exaggerated stock of finished goods or work in progress - goods	
Falsification of costing	
Incorrect physical inventory	
Significant cashable waste	
Significant discrepancies between the accounting balance and the response to the circulation request, inconsistencies, lack of response, refusal to send by the customer	
Detour of invoices or reminders	
Misappropriation of means of payment, payment without justification	
Significant discrepancies between accounting estimates and information from people other than management (accounting, external...)	
Non-completeness of accrued income or the opposite	
Tax calculation	
Large cash balances	
Handling of checks	
Double payments	
Improper use of the internal transfer account	
Large debit and credit movements in the accruals account with little or no final balance	
Expenses allocated too early or too late and other manipulations affecting the liability accounts	
Source of capital	
Difficult identification of the founders	
The disappearance of the amount paid in cash one or a few days after the payment	
A sudden and accentuated increase in equity in a rather unfavorable economic climate.	
Capital grants - forgery or negligence in amortization	
Over or undervaluation of provisions - cannot depend on the result of the year	
Existence of fictitious suppliers	

Recognition of actual expenses as a provision earlier than as an invoice receivable	
Increase in current account liabilities to directors	
Invoices for deliveries that in reality were never received or which do not represent the equivalent of the invoice amount	
Overvaluation of invoices receivable	
Remunerations are charged to the company for people who in reality work for other companies or who do not work at all.	
Fictitious employees	
Revenues are recorded as income while future obligations exist (advance payments)	
Income booked too early or too late or other manipulations before affecting the income statement	
Recognition of revenue for services not rendered - fraudulent invoicing	
Recognition of revenue from sales of goods not sent or not accepted by the customer	
Taking in result of a turnover corresponding to sales with unfulfilled contractual conditions	
A document that does not have the legal status of an invoice (e.g. commercial invoice) is recorded as a sale.	
Large influx or density of credit notes received or issued or disbursements from cash registers	
Turnover of goods that can still be returned	
Turnover of deliveries/services although it is known in advance that they will never be paid or even claimed	
Financing of the sale by the seller	
Inconsistency of the variations of the financial expenses and income about the other items	
Write-downs on current assets	
Extraordinary income and expenses are detailed enough that each amount draws attention and leads to justification.	
Recognition of questionable income in sales	
Transactions between related parties (group, staff, acquaintances, business partners...)	
A surprising similarity between the layout of the company's documents and those of the customers	
Accounting of money received as a sale	
A significant drop in customer demand	
Operating losses leading to fears of bankruptcy, closure or hostile takeover	
Fear of losing future contracts	
Little flexibility to meet listing obligations or debt covenants	
Dependence of the personal financial position of the directors or persons charged with governance on the entity's a performance / personal guarantee	
Significant transactions with related parties that are outside the scope of normal operations, or with related parties not audited or audited by another firm	
Existence of related parties in "tax havens	

Large, unusual or excessively complex transactions (substance over form)	
Significant foreign or international transactions in countries with different business practices and cultures	
Significant bank accounts, or transactions related to subsidiaries or branches in tax havens	
Disagreement between partners	
Unusual legal forms and reporting relationships	
Excessive involvement of non-financial executives in selecting accounting policies or making significant estimates	
Excessive concern by management for maintaining or increasing the stock price or earnings trend	
Large amounts of cash on hand or handled	
Insufficient computer literacy on the part of management, which allows computer specialists to commit misappropriations	
Indifference to the need to monitor or reduce risks related to asset misappropriation	
Lack of interest in internal controls to mitigate asset misappropriation	
Behavior that indicates dissatisfaction or unhappiness with the entity or the way it treats its employees	

A-5) Significance thresholds

A materiality threshold is "the limit below which an error made in good faith by the company does not affect the true and fair view of the financial statements, it being understood that the true and fair view is not limited to the regular entry in the balance sheet, but also depends on the importance that the reader of the accounts gives to obtaining the information" (Mikol, 1999). In the context of IFRS, it is also called the materiality threshold. It is the amount beyond which economic decisions or judgments based on the accounts are likely to be influenced.

First, the principle of materiality must be applied. The summary statements must reveal all elements whose significance may affect evaluations and decisions. Materiality is any information that is likely to influence the opinion that readers of the financial statements may have on the assets, financial situation, and results. According to IFAC (2009): "Materiality is defined in relation to the size or nature of a misstatement in the financial information, i.e. the auditor will assess both the amount and the nature of all misstatements identified". For this reason, the auditor should focus his or her work on items and transactions that are material. These transactions present a higher risk and allow the auditor to base his opinion on the true and fair view.

Therefore, setting materiality levels allows for better guidance and organization of the internal audit engagement by focusing on significant items and figures that exceed the materiality level.

The materiality level can be determined based on:
- Of the current result;
- Sales (e.g. x %);
- Net income (e.g. x %);
- Shareholders' equity (x %);
- Net debt.

It may also represent a combination of all of these elements and depend on the entity's industry. Materiality is a relative concept. In practice, auditors must assess a material misstatement on an individual basis and in the context of a company's overall financial statements. What constitutes a material misstatement for one company may not meet the materiality threshold for another. Materiality is a matter of professional judgment and experience of the audit team.

We have prepared a summary form for these choices related to materiality

Internal Audit of Treasury and cash management

presented in Form A-5: Materiality Levels for Treasury Accounts.
Form A-5: Treasury Account Materiality Threshold

"Company name"		Year : ....
A-5	**MATERIALITY THRESHOLD FOR CASH ACCOUNTS**	

OBJECTIVE
The objective is to determine the materiality level appropriately in the planning and execution of the audit.

STEP	Comments
Overall significance level	
Document and justify the overall materiality level set for the cash accounts as a whole.	
Threshold of significance for the execution of the work	
Other significance levels	
Document whether a different materiality threshold should be used for transaction flows, account balances, or disclosures.	
Insignificant threshold	
Document the threshold below which anomalies will be considered clearly insignificant	
Modification of the significance level	
Consider the need to change any of the above thresholds during the course of the audit due to final figures, changes in risk assessment, etc.	

A-6) The overall internal audit strategy

The internal auditor develops an audit grid that guides the audit strategy. An audit strategy specifies the categories of events related to account security. The internal auditor sets out the objective and risks, context, criteria, scope, and audit approach. The audit grid is a planning tool that can be used at this stage, as it helps to establish the audit strategy logically. It aims to align the various elements and highlight, from the outset, any obstacles to the audit. It is also used to communicate the key elements of the audit plan.

Planning is essential to ensure that the engagement is performed effectively and efficiently, and that audit risk has been reduced to an acceptably low level. The overall audit strategy begins with the risk assessment phase. The information gathered will be used to develop the detailed audit plan implementing the additional assertion-level procedures necessary to address the assessed risks.

We have established a grid of steps for the overall internal audit strategy for the treasury function, which is summarized in Form A-6: Audit Strategy Plan and Steps.

Internal Audit of Treasury and cash management

Form A-6: Overall Audit Strategy

"Company name"	Year : ....
A6	**Overall Audit Strategy**

OBJECTIVE				
The objective is to describe the steps necessary to develop the overall audit strategy.				
	Audit	Limited examination (or review)	Agreed procedures	Specific mission
Mission within the framework of the annual accounts				
Audit of financial information for the works council				
Assignment in the context of specific sector reporting requirements				

Comments and audit strategy	Significant risk Y/N
The company has one or more locations: The company has the following subsidiaries (name, % ownership): Are the subsidiaries audited?	

Internal Audit of Treasury and cash management

IMPORTANT FACTORS FOR THE AUDIT TEAM TO CONSIDER
Data from the previous audit (nature of the entity, internal control, type of audit opinion, significant risks, particular problems, etc.)

Comments and audit strategy	Significant risk Y/N
SIGNIFICANT CHANGES THAT MAY HAVE AN IMPACT ON THE AUDIT APPROACH	

Comments and audit strategy	Significant risk Y/N	Update	Initials	Date
New products or services				
Acquisitions, mergers, and divestitures				
Change in management personnel				
IT and business process change				

B) Detailed audit of the cash cycle

B-1) Segregation of duties grid:

According to Renard (2006), the task separation grid is a snapshot of the distribution of work at a given moment. It also provides an analysis of the workload of each person. It is a diagnostic tool that makes it possible to notice violations of the separation of duties, analyze the workload per agent, and to identify its structure. Its main purpose is to detect possible incompatibilities or overlapping tasks.

For the treasury function, a grid can be designed that will include a unitary breakdown of all operations related to this function. The objective is to highlight any overlapping tasks between incompatible functions.

Thus, we can distinguish, theoretically, five main incompatible functions within a company:
- The decision-making function: this is the power to initiate operations;
- The function of holding values and goods: This function can concern the people who have access to them as part of an operating process;
- The recording function: The capture and processing of information, generally this function is related to the accountants;
- The control function: Its objective is to verify the execution and methods of the other functions;
- The financial function: To be able to commit the expenses and collect the receipts of the company.

We have presented a grid for the separation of tasks. This form will be filled in after individual interviews with the respective operational staff according to their tasks. The form is in Form B-1: Segregation of duties form.

Internal Audit of Treasury and cash management

Functions	People involved								
	Purchasing manager	Warehouse manager	Accounting department	Chief Accountant	IT department	Financial director	Department concerned	HRD	DG
15. Maintenance of accounts payable	"Company name"				Year :				

B1	Segregation of duties grid

Form B-1: Segregation of Duties Chart

OBJECTIVE
The objective is to present the tasks related to the management of the treasury while taking care to verify the cases of incompatibility or conflict of services.

Functions	People involved								
	Purchasing manager	Warehouse manager	Accounting department	Chief Accountant	IT department	Financial director	Department concerned	HRD	DG
1. Buyer's request									
2. Request for Quotation									
3. Comparison table of offers									
4. Establishment of orders									
5. Order Authorization									
6. Receipt									
7. Quantity and quality control									
8. Comparison of order and delivery note									
9. Comparison of order and invoice									
10. Receipt slip - invoice comparison									
11. Accounting allocation									
12. Verification of the accounting allocation									
13. Payment voucher									
14. Maintenance of the purchase journal									

Internal Audit of Treasury and cash management

16. Reconciliation of supplier statements with accounts									
17. Signing of cheques									
18. Mailing of cheques									
19. Keeping the cash journal									
20. Access to general accounting									
21. Credit notes follow-up									
22. Access control									
23. Error correction									
24. Cheque book holding									
25. Maintenance of accounts receivable									
26. Investment decision									
27. Inventory									
28. Depreciation									
29. Payroll Instructions									
30. Establishment of payslip									
31. Payment									

B-2) The internal control questionnaire

An internal control questionnaire is an essential tool for carrying out the detailed phase of the audit assignment. It is an analysis grid that allows the auditor to understand the level of risks and to provide an overall diagnosis of the internal control process and methods.

The main purpose of this questionnaire is to obtain a general description of the organizational system in force within the company. Thus, through a series of questions, the auditor will obtain information on the progress of a procedure, to know exactly what happens in practice. These questions are intended to provide the auditor with the tools to carry out a professional and independent observation that allows for an exhaustive look at the functioning of the audited entity.

The internal control questionnaire is a guide for the auditor to carry out his work program. It is therefore a methodological tool that allows recognizing:
- Internal controls implemented in the past;
- Current audit objectives.

To achieve these two objectives, the internal control questionnaire should be composed of appropriate and targeted questions. The objective is to make an overall assessment of the treasury procedure. Also, we will obtain information on the progress of the payment and collection procedure by the treasury function, to know the reality of the methods or tools used in practice.

For our internal audit mission, we have designed an internal control questionnaire presented in Form B-2: Internal Control Questionnaire.

Internal Audit of Treasury and cash management

Form B-2: The Internal Control Questionnaire

"Company name"		Year : ....
B-2	The Internal Control Questionnaire	

OBJECTIVE
The main purpose of this questionnaire is to have a general description of the organization system in force within the company.

RISK RELATED TO THE GENERAL INTERNAL CONTROL ENVIRONMENT	TESTS YES/NO	RISk H/M/L	Observations
Did the audits of previous years reveal the existence of numerous internal control weaknesses?			
Is there a shortcoming in the organization plan, which may be reflected in the absence of an organization chart and a procedures manual?			
Have certain situations or events come to light that suggest the existence of fraud or errors leading to material misstatement of the accounts?			
Do one or more checks and balances limit management's full authority?			
Is management aware of the need for effective internal control?			
RISK RELATED TO THE ACCOUNTING AND IT SYSTEM	YES/NO	H/M/L	Observations
Is the accounting system rigorously maintained?			
Is the accounting staff properly trained?			
Are there budgets?			
Is there a regular comparison between budgets and achievements?			
Does the company use the services of a chartered accountant?			
Does management have control over the IT function?			
Is the software used to process accounting and financial information unreliable?			

Internal Audit of Treasury and cash management

SALES/CUSTOMER CYCLE: RISK ASSESSMENT	YES/NO	H/M/L	Observations
Are all sales recorded real and properly accounted for?			
Are there internal sales orders?			
Are they pre-numbered?			
Are numbered invoices sequentially numbered?			
Are undelivered orders tracked?			
Are these orders valued on a regular basis?			
STOCK CYCLE / RISK ASSESSMENT	YES/NO	H/M/L	Observations
Is the warehouse function separate from administrative functions?			
Is access to the stock sufficiently regulated?			
Is the physical protection of the stock sufficient?			
Is inventory adequately insured?			
Are put-away tickets used?			
Are stock release slips used?			
Do release slips have an authorized signature?			
Are there satisfactory physical inventory procedures?			
Is a perpetual inventory in place?			
If perpetual inventory exists, are the results of the physical inventory reconciled with the perpetual inventory?			
Are discrepancies investigated?			
Can the unit prices used to value the inventory be easily justified?			
CAPITAL CYCLE / RISK ASSESSMENT	YES/NO	H/M/L	Observations
Are there any studies prior to the acquisition of the assets?			
Are there capital budgets?			
Is this budget reconciled to the investments made?			
Are fixed asset invoices filed separately?			
Is there a fixed asset file?			
Does this file allow for a link between the amounts in the account and the existing ones?			
Are fixed assets inventoried regularly?			
If so, are the results reconciled to the file?			
Is there a maintenance department?			

Internal Audit of Treasury and cash management

	YES/NO	H/M/L	Observations
Are disposals and scraps approved?			
Are fixed assets adequately insured?			
Are fixed assets and depreciation records up to date?			
CASH CYCLE / RISK ASSESSMENT	**YES/NO**	**H/M/L**	**Observations**
Are the functional separations sufficient?			
Are payments received deposited promptly with the Bank?			
Are the payment vouchers pre-numbered?			
Is the numerical sequence of the payment vouchers on the treasury journal?			
Are vouchers canceled after payment to avoid double payments?			
Are accounts payable balances analyzed regularly to identify duplicate payments?			
Are bank reconciliations reviewed by a manager?			
Is cash on hand physically controlled and reconciled?			
Are payment vouchers pre-numbered?			
Is cash on hand maintained at a minimum level?			
Is a fixed-amount checkout system used?			
Is there regular monitoring of cash balances?			
Are the cash journals up to date?			
Are they regularly signed by a manager?			
Are bank reconciliation statements prepared regularly?			
Are these statements regularly cleared of old amounts?			
Does a competent and clearly defined manager regularly review the reconciliation statements?			
Are cash flow forecasts monitored regularly?			

Internal Audit of Treasury and cash management

PURCHASING/SUPPLIER CYCLE / RISK ASSESSMENT	YES/NO	H/M/L	Observations
Is there an authorization process for orders?			
Are open orders valued on a regular basis?			
Is the delivery subject to quality control?			
Are these checks documented?			
When invoices are received, is there an ORIGINAL stamp on one of the copies received?			
Are excess copies destroyed?			
Are the invoices reconciled with the receipt (or delivery) slips and purchase orders, in terms of quality?			
Is there a follow-up on credit notes?			
Do invoices include the accounting charge?			
Do the invoices include a visa for entry?			
Do the invoices include payment references?			
Do the invoices have a payment visa?			
Are the supplier's accounts up to date?			
Are payments made systematically based on a supporting document?			
Are the references to the paid invoices indicated on the payments to facilitate the lettering of the accounts ?			
PERSONAL CYCLE / RISK ASSESSMENT	YES/NO	H/M/L	Observations
Is there a procedure for hiring staff?			
Are the attendance times correctly known?			
Are the parameters used to establish the payroll properly controlled?			
Are parameter changes subject to a satisfactory authorization and control procedure?			
Are payroll items and payroll charges properly accounted for?			
Does the payment process include control of the amount paid to each employee by someone independent of payroll monitoring?			

B-3) The detailed plan of the cash flow audit

The development of a comprehensive internal audit plan should begin with a thorough understanding of the organization's objectives and business. Internal auditing should contribute to the achievement of the organization's strategic, operational, communication, and compliance objectives, while also assuring the preservation of the ethical environment and responsible culture.

The audit plan is a description of the activities and arrangements for conducting an audit. The content of the audit plan should be adjusted to the size and complexity of the company being audited.

It includes:
- The objectives of the audit;
- The areas of application of the audit;
- The place of this audit in the overall audit program;
- The identity of the audited companies or departments;
- The audit manager and auditors;
- Identification of reference documents;
- Date, duration and location of the audit.

We developed a detailed plan for the internal audit of the treasury function, which is presented in Form B-3: Detailed Treasury Audit Plan.

Form B-3: Detailed audit plan for cash and banks

"Company name"	Year : ....
B-3	DETAILED AUDIT PLAN CASH AND BANKS

OBJECTIVE
Respond to identified risks of material misstatement by obtaining appropriate and sufficient audit evidence to reduce audit risk to an acceptably low level.

	Treasury	Risks (high, medium, low) H, M, L	Comments
1.	**Analytical procedures**		
	• - Investigate significant changes in cash on hand and cash investments;		
	• - Test the relevance of interest expenses and/or financial income and correspondence with the average balance		
2.	**Bank confirmations for all accounts**		
	Existence of bank statements for the period.		
3.	**Review the bank reconciliation**		
	Ensure that bank statements match the trial balance and document unusual items.		
4.	**Subsequent payment**		
	Select disbursements over $1,000 to ensure that transactions are properly recorded in the correct period.		
5.	**Foreign currencies**		
	Ensure that all bank balances have been converted to the correct rate and period.		
6.	**Counting the cash**		
7	**Compliance with agreements**		
	Check that the entity is still in compliance with any covenants, cash withdrawal restrictions, minimum balance, etc.		

Internal Audit of Treasury and cash management

	"Company name"	Year : ....
B-3	DETAILED AUDIT PLAN FOR CASH AND BANKS	

OBJECTIVE
Respond to identified risks of a material misstatement by obtaining appropriate and sufficient audit evidence to reduce audit risk to an acceptably low level.

		Exhaustiveness	Existence	Accuracy	Valuation
Risk Response		H/M/L	H/M/L	H/M/L	H/M/L
A.	Basic procedure				
B.	Special procedures to address specific hazards.				
C.	Testing of procedures				
Comments					

Risk of material misstatement of the annual accounts as a whole: (high, medium, low)

Internal Audit of Treasury and cash management

	Treasury	Exhaustiveness	Existence	Accuracy	Valuation	Prepared by	reference	Comments
A.	**Basic procedures**							
1.	**Analytical procedures**							
	• - Investigate significant changes in cash on hand and cash investments; e.g., credit balances, abnormally high balances, and new and closed accounts.							
	• - Test the relevance of interest charges and/or financial income and correspondence with the average balance (monthly / quarterly).							
2.	**Bank confirmations for all accounts**							
	If there is a valid reason for not confirming the accounts, it must be justified in the working papers.							
3.	**Review the bank reconciliation**							
	Ensure that bank statements match the trial balance and document unusual items.							
	Treasury	Exhaustivene	Existence	Accuracy	Valuation	Prepared by	reference	Comments
4.	**Subsequent payment**							
	Select disbursements >_ $ after the closed period and ensure that the transactions are correctly recorded in							

	the correct period.							
5.	**Foreign currencies**							
	Ensure that all bank balances have been converted to the correct rate and period.							
6.	**Counting the cash**							
	Cash transactions							
	Assess the extent of cash deposits and payments by reviewing cash deposits, cash disbursements, and cash checks.							
7	**Compliance with agreements**							
	Verify that the entity is still in compliance with these possible covenants, possible cash withdrawal restrictions, minimum balance during the period and document violations, their resolution, and possibly if ongoing, future plans.							
	Special procedures to address specific risks.							
	Test procedures							

Initial each assertion to indicate that the planned audit response is sufficient to mitigate the assessed level of risk and the identified significant risk.

COMMENTS

Internal Audit of Treasury and cash management

ACTIVITY	Identified risk	Risk of fraud	Impact (a)	Probability (b)	Combined risk (a)*(b)
Separation of functions	Unauthorized or fraudulent transactions may occur due to poor segregation of duties in the treasury and investment department				
Basic file management	Changes or additions can be made to the base files by unauthorized persons				
	The data in the master files could be wrong				
	Other (to be defined)				
Cash and liquidity management	Invalid cash transactions can be executed (checks, transfers)				
	Cash transactions are not correctly or fully recorded in the appropriate period				
	Unauthorized cash transactions can occur				
	Possibility of overriding controls				
	Unauthorized transactions may occur				
	Cash payments over $3,000 can be accepted				
	Unauthorized transfers exceeding payment limits may occur				
	Transfer to a subcontractor with social debts				
	Other (to be defined)				
Physical protection	Valuable documents are misused or stolen				
	Cash register differences				
	Différences entre les caisses enregistreuses				
	Other (to be defined)				

ACTIVITY	Identified risk	Risk of fraud	Impact (a)	Probability (b)	Combined risk (a)*(b)
Investments	Differences between cash registers				
	Investments are not properly or fully recorded in the appropriate period				
	Unauthorized transactions may occur				
	Investments are authorized outside the budget				
	Other (to be defined)				
Debt management	Unauthorized activities may occur				
	Intercompany loans are not correct or not accounted for in the correct period				
	Unauthorized debts may be incurred				
	Inadequate debt repayments or interest payments are made				
	Other (to be defined)				
Financial reporting and control	Cash transactions may not be recorded in the appropriate period				
	Financial reporting may contain errors				
	Some transactions may be processed or recorded incorrectly				
	Other (to be defined)				

Desirable Internal Controls and points of attention related to internal control	Description of internal control	Ref doc	Evaluation of the control	Residual risk
The following functions must be separated - Approval of transactions - Transaction execution - Transaction posting - Confirmation and reconciliation Updating master files				
User access is consistent with the segregation of duties				
Access to master files is limited to authorized persons				
There is a procedure for validating changes to the file to prevent incorrect data from being entered into the system.				
There is a reporting system for changes in the master files that are verified with the master documents				
The master files are periodically checked by management.				
Cash transactions are checked and approved by an appropriate person.				
Payment limits are determined by an appropriate person				
Cash transactions are reviewed and approved by an appropriate person before posting				
The ability to open, modify or close bank accounts is limited to authorized persons				
Access to cash management is limited to authorized persons				
The signing of checks is limited to authorized persons				
Check signing authority is established and approved				
The cash management system prevents transactions from being processed when specific authorized limits are exceeded				
The ability to make transfers is limited to authorized persons				
Access to cash management is limited to authorized persons.				
Authorization limits have been assigned to those responsible for approving transfers.				
Cash transactions are monitored and approved by an appropriate person.				
The system for transfers prevents transactions from being processed when the limits defined for a specific person are exceeded.				

Internal Audit of Treasury and cash management

Additional approval is required so that transactions exceeding the limits defined for a specific person can still be processed.				
Information on the debts of subcontractors is obtained regularly				
Only authorized persons have access to valuable documents				
Daily cash counting				
The transport and protection of cash is carried out by suitable persons and bodies				
Approval limits are set for appropriate and authorized persons				
Investments are checked and approved by an appropriate person before being posted				
The ability to open, modify or close credit lines is limited to authorized persons				
The ability to decide to invest is limited to authorized persons				
Defined limits have been allocated to those responsible for approving investments				
Procedures for the execution of investments prevent the processing of transactions when the limits defined for a specific person are exceeded.				
Additional approval is required so that transactions exceeding the limits defined for a specific person can still be processed.				
The transaction journal entry is reviewed and approved by an appropriate person before posting				
An appropriate person approves intercompany borrowings				
The commitment to debt is limited to authorized individuals				
Management controls and approves the repayment of debts to ensure that repayments are made when due and by the terms of the commitments				
General ledger accounts for financial resources, investments and liabilities are reconciled regularly with external confirmations				
Management reporting on investments is reviewed and approved by the appropriate level of management				
Intercompany balances are reviewed and reconciled monthly				
Management reporting on investments is reviewed and approved by the appropriate level of management				

B-4) Treasury control: Compliance tests on the expenditure system

The main purpose of the cash flow audit is to diagnose:
- Payments made and their respective accounting records;
- The adequacy of the recording period;
- Payments and receipts relate to real and justified elements of the enterprise;
- The elements of the assets are adequately valued.

For the development of this cash flow control, we can opt for a test on a representative sample of documents and accounting records. We can choose the largest amounts, amounts that are similar, repeated numbers, or the most important customers or suppliers. We can identify information that will make our control easier. This control is detailed on three levels: a control of cash expenditures, a control of domestic payments, and a control of international payments.

The procedure relating to the expenditure fund:
The cash register can only be charged using expenditure orders presented to the cashier. Generally, the amounts passed through the cash register are small amounts. These payments can also be linked to expenses of an urgent nature. For example, the payment of daily transportation costs for brokers or the purchase of small supplies. It is also necessary to examine the application of the procedures laid down in the manual of procedures concerning payments by cash. Finally, we can verify that the amount recorded in the accounts corresponds unquestionably to the voucher and that the expense is related to the operation of the company.

The procedure for national payments

For domestic payments, the treasurer has the option of using several bank accounts in domestic currency and also of converting existing foreign currency assets into another convertible account. It is also a matter of working on a representative sample of accounting documents by carrying out document checks, arithmetic checks, verification of the accounting record, and the relationship of the expenditure to the company's operating needs.

The procedure for international payments

The specificity of this procedure is due to the legal framework of international payments and also to the importance of these payments given their amounts and given the discounts that can be earned. At the control level, we can verify the adequacy of the accounting documents with the requirements of international payments in terms of the presence of the original invoice, the delivery note, the purchase order, the import notice, and also the transfer order sent to the bank.

The data relating to these three controls are summarized in Form B-4: Compliance Tests on the Expenditure System (National, International, and Cash).

Internal Audit of Treasury and cash management

Form B-4: Test of the cash register, transfer of national and international suppliers

"Company name"	Year : ....
B-4	Test of the expense account

OBJECTIVE
Ensure that cash expenditures are real, documented and authorized by line management.

Reality testing on the cash register:

Date	Label	Amount	Verification with the supporting document	Operating Expense	Existence of an expense order	Affixing of the payment stamp

Points raised: (examples)

Several non-operating expenses

Partial presence of expense orders

The opposition to payment stamps in the various documents

The problem in the filing of certain accounting documents

Internal Audit of Treasury and cash management

	"Company name"	Year : ....
B-4		Tests on national supplier transfers

OBJECTIVE
Ensure that expenditures for domestic vendor payments are actual, supported by documentation, and authorized by line management.

Reality check on national supplier transfers:

Date	Label	Amount	Verification with the supporting document	Operating Expense	Existence of an expense order	Affixing of the payment stamp

Points raised: (examples)

Presence of supporting documents

Majority of expenses related to the operation

Presence of photocopies of cheques

Filing problem

Internal Audit of Treasury and cash management

"Company name"		Year : ....
B-4		Tests on international supplier transfers

OBJECTIVE
Ensure that foreign vendor expenses are real, documented and authorized by line management.

Reality check on international supplier transfers:

Date	Label	Amount	Verification with the supporting document	Operating Expense	Existence of an expense order	Affixing of the payment stamp

Points raised: (examples)

Presence of all invoices, delivery notes, and import notices

Total expenses related to the operation (purchase of raw materials)

Presence of expense orders

Loss of certain discounts and invoices for price complements.

B-5) Continuity testing on the preparation and verification of bank reconciliation statements

The bank reconciliation is a comparison between the accounting of the bank that keeps the bank account and the accounting of the company (the bank account kept by the company). As a result of this comparison, discrepancies may appear.

You should first obtain the bank reconciliation statements from the banks, prepared by the company, and verify that:
- They are confirmed regularly at the end of each month;
- The balance at the bank matches the balance on the bank statement;
- Arithmetic balances are correct;
- All reconciliation statements are signed by the person who prepared them and approved by a manager in the accounting department.

The bank reconciliation statement is a central part of the internal control process. Every difference and every discrepancy must be explained and corrected. Adjustment is mandatory.

Here are some possible controls during the post-control with a bank reconciliation: first, you have to make sure of the arithmetic control. Indeed, a bank reconciliation. Secondly, one must check for bank suspense items that appear abnormal or illogical. These are, for example, cash payments of large amounts, checks that have not been cashed for a very long period, or pending operations for abnormally small amounts. Finally, retrieve supporting documents for a control sample to understand the accounting logic (accounting document, notice, invoice, etc.).

We have designed a permanence test delivered in Form B-5: Permanence test on the elaboration of bank reconciliation statements.

Form B-5: Completeness and Compliance Testing of Bank Reconciliation Statements

"Company name"	Year : ....
B-5	**Completeness and compliance testing of bank reconciliation statements**

OBJECTIVE
Ensure that reconciliation statements are regularly prepared.

Source: Bank reconciliation statements for the audited year.

Month	Account 1	Account 2	Account 3	Account 4
1				
2				
3				
4				
5				
6				
7				
8				
9				

E: Audited and Balanced Reconciliation Statement

N: Audited and unbalanced reconciliation statement

T: Unaudited and non-existent reconciliation statement

B-6) Document Control

Documentary control refers to the use of supporting accounting documents to validate the control. These documents can be external (e.g. supplier's invoice, bank statement) or internal (internal document). In terms of evidence, external documents are more conclusive than internal documents.

Accounting information has different degrees of reliability. The notion of document refers directly to the notion of writing, support, and traceability, authenticity, and identification system. An integral part of the internal audit, without which it could not be properly performed and validated. Indeed, the decisive force of the information is increasing according to this order:
1. Verbal information
2. Review of internal documents
3. Review of a third party document
4. Direct confirmation from a third party
5. Physical observation

We can opt for an examination of the internal documents through a global analysis of the accounting documents and the accounting records of the bank account. Form B-6: Control of bank account documents.

Internal Audit of Treasury and cash management

Form B-6: Bank Account Document Control

"Company name"	Year : ....
B-6	Control of the documents of the account Bank

OBJECTIVE
Ensure that the Bank X account documents are present and complete.

Account	
Folder	
From	
A	

Item	Missing	Comments
1		
2		
3		
4		
5		
6		
7		
8		

B-7) Third-party confirmation

Third parties are generally banks, suppliers, customers, insurance companies, lawyers, notaries, etc. This third party will then send the requested information directly to the internal auditor. This procedure allows the auditor to have information from a different and more reliable source. He will then be able to compare and evaluate this information with that which he has obtained in the company. This comparison will allow the auditor to have an assurance of the reality and the completeness of the elements recorded in the accounts.

Confirmation requests with third parties can be closed or open. For example, it is possible to ask a customer for the amount due to the company on a given date. Generally, confirmation requests to customers are closed, those to suppliers and banks are open.

The procedure is to send a confirmation request. Here is an example of a confirmation request to a supplier to check the amount due on a given date. This request is inserted in Form B-7: Third-Party Confirmation.

Internal Audit of Treasury and cash management

Form B-7: Third-Party Confirmation

"Company name"	Year : ....
B-7	**Third Party Confirmation.**

OBJECTIVE
Ask a supplier for the amount remaining to be paid by the company at a given date.

" First and last name "

....

                                                Date: ....

Supplier: ....

Dear Sir/Madam;

In the course of our regular examination of the account of the above Company, we find that the balance on your account is as follows:

Balance at: September X, XXXX	Due to you: USD XX XXX

If the above balance on the date mentioned is correct please confirm by signing this letter where indicated and returning it to us.

If you do not agree to the above balance, we should be grateful if you could write directly to us and give details of the difference.

Yours faithfully,

Détails of the difference, if any:	Balance Confirmed :

                                                          (Please sign here)

B-8) The Payment Dashboard

The dispersion of accounting documents is one of the first causes of late payment. By centralizing invoices and payments, you can reduce the risk of forgetting an invoice.

The dashboard is used to manage the company or the project in question; to make informed decisions based on objective data measured on it. Management dashboards are a valuable tool.

They allow you to make and develop financial forecasts, which are essential for:
- Set realistic objectives in terms of turnover,
- Anticipate an increase in workload,
- Anticipate the launch of a new activity or the recruitment of a new employee,
- Anticipate cash flow problems,
- Negotiate an overdraft or other short-term financial solutions with your banker,
- Negotiate fundraising with investors,
- Maintaining the overall performance of the company (Bentalha et al., 2020), etc.

Today's accounting software has been shaped by digital transformation. As businesses grow, cash flow management becomes increasingly complex and can be difficult to track. To keep track of expenses, it is possible to set up an electronic invoice archive.

A supplier invoice tracking table can be created. You can also create a customer invoice tracking table. In both cases, the table must have a column for each piece of information:
- Name of the third party
- Invoice number
- Invoice date
- Due date
- Invoice amount
- Days overdue
- Amount of surcharge
- Balance due

- Payment status
- Dates of reminders sent

In addition, at the end of each month, a global statement of the payments made can be established to identify the global amounts and compare them between the different periods (Form B-8: The Payments Dashboard).

Internal Audit of Treasury and cash management

Form B-8: The Payment Dashboard

"Company name"	Year : …………..
B-8	The Payment Dashboard

Days	Payments			
	Suppliers	Gross amount	Commission	Net amount
(…)				
11				
11				
11				
11				
	(…..)			

TOTAL PAYMENTS / Month
XXXXXXXXX

BANK
STATEMENT Bank xx/xx/xxxx

DAYS	debited account	account credited
SI		
3		
3		
3		
3		
5		
5		
(…)		

Internal Audit of Treasury and cash management

Bank reconciliation	
PAYMENT	Bank statement

Summary of the Payment Table
Bank balance
....
....
REMAINDER TO PAY
....
NET BALANCE
....
UPCOMING PAYMENT
....
NEED NEXT PERIOD
....

B-9) Treasury reporting

Cash flow reporting and forecasts enable the company's cash performance to be managed to better understand business cycles, anticipate risks, guide operational investment choices and contribute to strategic thinking.

Cash flow monitoring reporting can include:
- Indicators for liquidity management
- Indicators for risk management
- Other indicators
- Organization of reporting

An efficient management reporting tool allows you to obtain real-time figures by simply updating the data. In addition, for companies with several liquidity accounts, the tool provides an overall picture of the financial situation and establishes real-time control.

Internal Audit of Treasury and cash management

"Company name"	Year : ....
B-9	Cash Flow Reporting

Form B-9: Cash-Flow Reporting

Bank and Cash Report

Company Code		Company
Currency Code		xxxx
Year		
Month		
Actual		

(Please use for each bank account one row.)

Bank Category	Bank Name	Bank account number/IBAN	Partner Bank Account	Cash & Cash Equivalent
Other Banks				
Other Banks				
Other Banks				
Other Banks				
Other Banks				
Other Banks				
Other Banks				
Cash				

B-10) Bank commission tracking form

The form for monitoring bank commissions and fees makes it possible to know the amount of money that the bank collects for products and services in the context of managing the bank account. Bank charges represent the price paid by a client for the performance of a transaction, the supply of a product, or the provision of a service.

The summary distinguishes:
- Fees for memberships or subscriptions to various products or services;
- Fees paid for the performance of a transaction or in exchange for the provision of a product or service;
- Fees related to the operation of these different products and services;
- Charges related to payment incidents and other irregularities (overdraft fees, cheque or direct debit rejection fees, etc.).

Some bank fees are regulated and capped. The others are freely fixed by the establishment. The monthly total of bank charges as well as the ceiling of the overdraft authorization, if any, must appear on the account statement. A detailed summary of the fees charged by the bank for the management of the account must also be sent each period.

The analysis and optimization of these bank charges are essential for the cash flow audit. For this reason, it is necessary to make a detailed monthly table of commissions and bank charges. This involves analyzing the total amount paid, the largest commissions, the repeated amounts, and ensuring the accuracy of the calculations and the banker's fees (Form B-10: Bank Commission Tracking Form).

Internal Audit of Treasury and cash management

"Company name"	Year : …………..
B-10	**Bank Commission Tracking Form**

Form B-10: Bank Commission Tracking Form

Month: …………..

Status Commissions ……

ACCOUNT	Month	TOTAL COMMISSION
xxxx		
	Total	
	Average	

Correction of commissions				
Date	Operation	Amount	Comment	Correction

Internal Audit of Treasury and cash management

B-11) Currency conversion form

When a company carries out commercial transactions in a currency that is not its national currency, it is subject to changes in exchange rates, which will ultimately impact its profitability and cash flow. These are common transactions for exporting and importing companies. These variations in currency rates can have both a positive and negative impact on the commercial margin. This is what we call the exchange rate risk.

Not managing this risk can result in a loss of profit for the company, even if the exchange rate fluctuation is positive. The company is constantly evolving in an uncertain environment. Especially for small businesses, it is impossible to predict what the profits will be on each transaction or what cash flow they will have to fulfill the next contract.

Managing cash flow for a company that operates internationally with multiple currencies can be particularly challenging. For companies that work with multiple currencies daily basis, bank accounts that are based in foreign currencies must be integrated. The information is then automatically converted into national currency and consolidated with the rest of the cash flow. It is also necessary to verify that the exchange rates used are correct and that the treasurer can carry out the conversion operations under the best conditions. The internal control of these operations includes compliance with the standards in force, respect for the legal frameworks of these operations, and also the ability of the executor to have the best financial or banking conditions.

Internal Audit of Treasury and cash management

Form B-11: Currency Conversion Form

"Company name"	Year : ....
B-11	Currency conversion form

Month: ....

Days	Time	Currency	Conversion rate used	Current conversion rate	Operators

Currency: ....

B-12) Discount follow-up

A commercial discount is a discount that is made directly between a company and its customer or its supplier. It consists in proposing to the third party to settle its invoice before the due date in return for a discount. It does not require to pass by a bill of exchange. It is a means used by certain companies to increase their available cash while benefiting from a good image with their customers.

A commercial discount is a financing tool. It offers the advantage for the company to improve its cash flow without going through a banking partner. It is generally less expensive than bank financing. Invoice discounting can also be used as a loyalty tool. Within the framework of a long relationship with a customer, the company can make a commercial gesture and offer him an invoice discount.

The control of these discount operations can be vital, especially for importing companies, given the amounts transited. This control aims at validating the adequacy of the operations carried out with the rules traced, the respect of the regulatory frameworks, and also the ability of the accountant or the treasurer to obtain the discounts, to grant the discounts respecting the limits and the conditions traced and finally, to verify the adequacy of these discounts with the commercial and financial policy.

Internal Audit of Treasury and cash management

"Company name"		Year : ....
B-12		**Discount follow-up**

Form B-12: Follow-up of Discounts

Follow-up of balances

Date	Operation	ESCOMPT .... (Obtained or granted)	Max	Min	Amount	Limit

CORRECTION OF DISCOUNTS

Date	Operation	ESCOMPT .... (Obtained or granted)	Error	Correction	Comment

C/ The audit summary phase

The memorandum summarizes the audit process involved in issuing the internal auditor's opinion. As such, the design of the memorandum does not require any new information. It, therefore, takes information from the various forms already established.

There are several points of closure of the audit engagement that can be presented:

1. Review of evidence found;
2. Assessment of the company's legal issues;
3. Summary of the mission:
- The evaluation of anomalies found during the audit;
- The drafting of the summary note presented to the Management;
- The areas of progress of the mission.
- Formulation of the opinion

To present the results, we worked with two annexes as follows:
Form C-1: Summary of Major Findings and Form C-2: Audit Completion Review.

Internal Audit of Treasury and cash management

Form C1 : Summary of major findings during the mission

"Company name"		Year : ....
C-1	**SUMMARY OF MAJOR FINDINGS DURING THE MISSION**	
OBJECTIVE		
The objective is to summarize the nature of the significant problems encountered and the related decisions made during the mission.		

N°	Description of the problem or audit finding	Nature of the decision required
1		
2		
3		
4		
5		
6		
7		
8		
9		
10		

Form C1 : Summary of major findings during the mission (Examples)

	"Company name"	Year : ....
C-1	SUMMARY OF MAJOR FINDINGS DURING THE MISSION	
OBJECTIVE		
The objective is to summarize the nature of the significant problems encountered and the related decisions made during the mission.		

N°	Description of the problem or audit finding	The nature of the decision required
1	Lack of an internal audit or internal control function	Possibility to create an internal audit function
2	Payment to local suppliers without considering the effect on tax recovery	Need for the training of accountants in terms of taxes and especially the suspensive regime
3	Lack of entry endorsement on payments	Introduce a Visa to pay or make a monthly follow-up for each supplier
4	Delayed payment and loss of discount for foreign suppliers	Divide the foreign suppliers into two categories according to the discount and pay the foreign suppliers with the discount 10 days in advance to avoid delays of payment caused by the international transfers between the banks
5	Problems in evaluating the exchange rate for international payments	Review the method of calculating the average exchange rate and correct the accounting records
6	Possibility of current account deficits for foreign currency payments	Establish a cash flow statement in national currency and in foreign currency to make accurate forecasts of the amounts to be paid
7	Problems in estimating exchange rate differences and provisions for exchange rate risk	Draw up a summary calculation table distinguishing between the possible cases of clients, suppliers, advances, etc.

N°	Description of the problem or audit finding	The nature of the decision required
8	High amounts paid by the cashier	Set a maximum amount for cash payments by the third party and by period
9	Existence of several invoices not related to operations	Review certain expenses with the sales department, given the nature of these expenses not related to operations.
10	Absence of certain supporting documents (photocopies or filing problems)	Ask the bank for certain documents or suppliers (duplicates). Also, review the filing procedure and the people involved in this procedure.
11	Inaccuracy of certain bank reconciliations	Control of bank reconciliations and management approval
12	Weaknesses in cash flow forecasts	Daily treasury TDB/ Online balance consultation
13	Insufficiently parameterized software	Need to request access to software for example for the case of accounting entry templates.
14	No procedure for negotiating banking conditions	Creation of an analysis of bank costs and agios
	(...)	

Internal Audit of Treasury and cash management

Form C2: Audit Review and Completion

"Company name"	Year : ....
C-2	**Audit Review and Completion**

OBJECTIVE
The objective is to describe the various requirements for establishing, modifying, and maintaining audit documentation. The auditor must prepare audit documentation to ensure that he/she has performed the audit in accordance with International Standards on Auditing and applicable legal and regulatory requirements and that he/she has obtained sufficient appropriate audit evidence on which to base his/her opinion on the true and fair view of the financial statements.

	Yes/No	Comments
ACCEPTANCE/CONTINUITY/MAINTENANCE		
1. Have independence, ethical or other acceptance risks been resolved?		
2. Have the procedures for accepting or continuing the engagement been performed (e.g., scope, planning, understanding the entity, interviewing the audit team, describing significant risks, describing internal control, going concern, communicating internal control weaknesses to management, etc.)?		
3. Has this strategy been documented by the following key documents? • audit planning memorandum and work program • team planning meeting • minutes of discussions with the team and management on fraud issues • documentation of communication with those constituting corporate governance • documentation of communication of internal control weaknesses • risk matrix • calculation of materiality, etc.		

Internal Audit of Treasury and cash management

RISK EVALUATION			
4.	Has a comprehensive audit strategy been completed and documented?		
RISK ASSESSMENT			
5.	Has our understanding of the entity been documented and updated?		
RISK ASSESSMENT			
6.	Have material weaknesses in internal control been identified and reported to management?		
RISK RESPONSES			
7.	Were the additional audit procedures performed sufficient and appropriate to address the assessed risks and thereby reduce the audit risk to an acceptable low level?		
REPORT			
8.	Is the auditor's report appropriately formulated in light of the nature of the engagement and the evidence obtained?		
9.	Are post-closing events adequately reflected in the annual accounts and the date of the audit report?		
10.	Have there been any meetings with management		
11.	Have notes of significant decisions and details of possible adjustments not accepted by management been documented?		

Internal Audit of Treasury and cash management

CASH FLOW AUDIT CHECKLIST		
12. Procedures Do you have well-documented operating procedures in place (front, middle and back office)? Can you validate the use or benchmarking of your procedures? Is your team informed and fully aware of your procedures? What measures do you have in place to cover short or extended staff leaves? Do you have a visible business continuity plan? Do you have evidence that the effects have been tested? Does your effect cover day-to-day operational risks? Do you have error reporting measures in place?		
13. Segregation of duties Is the segregation of duties adequate and non-overlapping between functions? Is there adequate segregation of duties with no overlap between functions? Do you have a cash management system? Do you have sufficient knowledge of the cash management system internally?		
14. Independence Do you use independent assessments? Do you use a third-party execution platform and does your team have knowledge and control of the results? Control of results?		
15. Cash management system Is your cash management system fit for purpose? Does your cash management system ensure data integrity? Do you have processes in place to ensure the integrity of the data entered? Do you understand the methodologies of your cash management system (e.g. transaction valuation)? Do you understand the reporting functionality of your cash management system? Are you using all of its features?		

Internal Audit of Treasury and cash management

In this chapter, we have presented the objectives and the methodology chosen for the internal audit of the treasury cycle. Our main objective is to build an internal audit model specific to the treasury function. The aim is to create a global and integrated procedure to improve the company's performance through an internal audit of the treasury cycle. The construction of this analysis model is carried out using pre-established, numbered, and ordered forms, the objective of which is to guide the internal auditor's approach.

The internal auditor can also use a checklist to verify his or her treasury audit assignment. The verification and systemic application of our approach have enabled us to identify several points for further study, which we will present in the next chapter.

CHAPTER 3
RECOMMENDATIONS AND PERSPECTIVES OF THE INTERNAL AUDIT OF THE TREASURY CYCLE

The internal audit allows for the identification of several points. The originality of the work lies in the integrated design of the analysis model based on the internal audit forms created and specific to the audit of the cash cycle, detailing the methodology presented and the method to be pursued.

The results obtained must be discussed with the General Management in a closing meeting. The internal auditor will present the results of the investigations and the corrections to be taken into consideration. The results obtained can also be completed by recommendations and perspectives to be implemented for the company in the short and long term.

The recommendations are an important part of the final audit work. This is the final stage of the internal audit. For this reason, recommendations are an important component of the final audit report.

Overall performance indicators (Bentalha et al., 2020; Hmioui and Bentalha, 2020) are needed to validate the quality of the recommendations made by the internal auditor. For this reason, the recommendations represent signals to assess the effectiveness of the internal audit. The approach is therefore qualitative, not quantitative. A recommendation is the expression of a measure aimed at reinforcing the effectiveness of control. There may be several solutions and corrective measures to correct a given malfunction. The choice of the corrective measure that will be the subject of the recommendation will be determined by considerations of cost, speed of implementation, ease of execution, etc.

The relevance and consistency of the internal auditor's conclusions can be assessed based on the following indicators:
- Percentage of recommendations completed;
- Timeliness of recommendations;
- Consistency of the recommendations with the overall objective and with each other.

At the end of the audit, several recommendations may be made to management. Some examples are as follows:
- Possibility of creating a specific internal audit function in the audited company;
- Need for dedicated training for accountants;
- Introduce a Visa (in the form of a stamp) to pay or do a monthly follow-up for each national and foreign supplier;
- Review the method of calculating the exchange rate;
- Establish a cash flow statement in national and foreign currency to make accurate forecasts of the amounts to be paid each month;
- Set a maximum amount for cash payments by the third party and by period;
- Review certain expenses with the sales department, given the nature of these expenses not related to operations.
- Authorize accountants to refuse payments when the designation on the invoices is not precise or missing;
- Ask the bank for certain documents or suppliers (duplicates) to complete certain files;
- Review the filing procedure by putting files by period and specify the participants in this procedure by limiting access;
- Control of bank reconciliations by a line manager and put a visa of the management after each month;
- Provide a daily cash flow statement and an online balance consultation;
- Need to request access to the software for example for the case of accounting entry models;
- Creation of a form for the analysis of bank costs and agios.

The internal auditor must follow up on the implementation of the actions envisaged based on the recommendations made. The validation and closing meeting should present several objectives:

- o   Present the findings;
- o   Explain the recommendations;
- o   Establish the action plan and the methodology for the follow-up of the mission.

The action plan makes it possible to control what is to be done and how it is done. Its main purpose is to:
- Allow for an exhaustive list of actions to be taken. This gives a global and detailed vision of the corrective actions;
- Optimize human and financial resources;
- To control the execution time of the corrective actions;
- To know our progress about the final vision of the corrective actions;
- To be able to find alternative solutions;
- Involve and motivate the teams by defining the roles of each one;
- To allow better coordination between the team members of each department in case of dependencies between actions.

The resources needed to implement each recommendation should be assessed. A person responsible for each corrective action should be appointed. The effective implementation of corrective actions is ensured by a rigorous allocation of resources and responsibilities. A due date should be established for each corrective action. The implementation schedule of the action plan should take into account the importance of the risks to be controlled and therefore the urgency to improve their control.

Changes in the progress of the improvement actions will lead to a periodic update of the action plan. The updated action plan must be communicated to the internal auditor. This form can be summarized as Form D- 1: Summary Action Plan for Cash Cycle Audit.

Form D-1: Summary action plan for the cash cycle audit

Procedure	Area of improvement	Horizon	People involved	Annexes

Form D-1: A summary action plan for the cash cycle audit (examples)

Procedure	Area of improvement	Horizon	People involved	Annexes
Insufficiently parameterized software	Request access and authorization from the software provider	Immediate	IT Department	
Monitoring of bank balances	Set up a cash flow monitoring dashboard for international payments	Immediate	International Payments Accountant	
Global cash flow reporting	Set up a summary statement of the global cash flow	Immediate	International Payments Accountant	
Cash control	Reduce the amounts paid by the cashier and set up a periodic follow-up	Short term	Cashier	
Follow-up of bank commissions	Establish a monthly statement for monitoring bank commissions by category	Short term	International and domestic payment accountant Domestic payments accountant	
Bank reconciliation	Decentralize the bank reconciliation by treasury officer and double sign each reconciliation	Short term	Chief Accountant	
Management of currency exchange conditions	Establish a statement for each currency conversion operation (negotiation)	Immediate		
Creation of an internal audit department	Set up an internal audit department	Long term	General Management	
	(…)			

Every audit mission ends with the drafting of a final audit report. The management must issue comments if it considers the action plan to be insufficient. The detailed audit report, for the attention of the auditees, must contain at least the following information:
- the purpose of the mission
- the scope of the mission (activities audited, period...)
- results (observations, conclusions, recommendations, action plan)

If the risk is accepted, an observation may not be subject to an action plan.

The report should also describe the auditor's method of follow-up to verify that corrective actions have been implemented.
A summary, for the attention of senior management, may include the following information:
- the results of the audit that have an impact on the entire organization
- An overall opinion, both positive and negative, on the ability of the audited area to control major risks.

This summary can be integrated into the audit report or be the subject of a separate note.
The internal audit of the treasury cycle must allow for an understanding of the internal functioning, to look for possible dysfunctions and the envisaged areas of improvement.

The detailed audit program is based on four levels of analysis. Firstly, an analysis of the current situation through a detailed diagnosis of the company's environment and the internal situation of the audited system. Second, an analysis of the accounts and procedures related to the cash cycle through a detailed diagnosis. Thirdly, a synthesis of the remarks and observations related to the points detected in the diagnosis. Fourthly, a proposal for correction and improvement through an action plan.

CONCLUSION

Internal auditing is one of the most topical themes in managerial and academic discussions. Indeed, after the financial crises and the complexity of the relations between shareholders and managers, internal auditing seems today to be both a research axis and a managerial practice of great interest. The activity of internal auditing creates added value and its main mission is to identify risks. Therefore, internal auditing must be at the service of the entire organization to make a real contribution to value creation and corporate governance.

It is by definition a:
- Activity: The ability of an internal audit organization to use external or internal service providers and a scientific sequence of the internal audit process;
- Assurance: It should be the process by which the organization ensures that risks are understood and managed appropriately.
- Advice: Verification, but also proposals and improvement paths;
- Risk: Not limited to financial, operational, and strategic risks, but also includes the non-exploitation of possible opportunities.

Internal auditing must be connected to the company, and be attached to its culture. Consequently, the internal audit can contribute to the analysis of the different departments and functions, including the company's cash flow. The cash flow is made up of the company's available cash and liquid assets. It is the difference between cash on hand and bank loans granted. The cash flow is at the center of all operations carried out by the company. It is the translation into the monetary form of all the company's decisions and operations. Cash management plays an active role in the company's results, a source of improvement in its profitability.

Every company must always have sufficient resources to meet its financial commitments. Otherwise, it will quickly run into payment difficulties or even default on payments and eventually be liquidated. For this reason, the audit of the cash cycle is of great importance for companies.

The primary objective of the cash cycle audit is to ensure that the company's cash position at the end of the financial year is accurately reflected. For this reason, the internal auditor must follow an orderly and scientific approach and also use a set of tools at his disposal. The digital revolution, the demands of social and societal responsibility, the need to innovate in an ultra-competitive sector... all these changes require skills and resources to manage the growing complexity and international competition.

Thus, we have presented in a theoretical and conceptual way the internal audit as a modern approach to performance management through the search for continuous improvement of the organization. Therefore, the audit of the cash flow cycle is essential given the importance of liquidity and financing choices and their direct impact on the performance and competitiveness of companies. Thus, we have presented in empirical form the internal audit of the cash cycle through a set of tools at our disposal and we have established forms prior to the internal audit.

Indeed, there is a close relationship between internal auditing and performance, given the positive impacts of internal auditing in terms of improving procedures, controlling and mastering operations, and formalizing work mechanisms and the behavior of actors. The major finding of this work is the importance of internal audit as a means of improving individual and collective performance of the company.

The proposed internal audit can allow the formalization of practical tools adapted to the audited entity and the design of an internal audit methodology specific to both the accounting and finance function and also specific to the company and its sector of activity. At the theoretical level, very few research works have focused on the cash cycle. The objective of our work is to enrich the academic and scientific debate on this specific audit given its importance for companies. At the methodological level, our approach has been to use a variety of modulated approaches such as questionnaires, interviews, observation and also a documentary study. The use of this set of tools allowed us to formalize audit forms specific to the cash flow audit, which gave a specificity to our methodological approach. At the managerial level, this work allowed us to set up a very efficient cash management system, in order to control the risks of insolvency and to be able to negotiate the banking conditions. Also, our work can be used by internal auditors as a methodical and professional tool for internal audit practices.

With this work, we wanted to participate scientifically in the improvement of the practice of internal auditing, so that it would produce a socio-economic added value. However, we do not claim that this is an exhaustive or complete work, as we had to face several limitations: methodological limitations, as we have designed tools specifically for the treasury function, whereas internal auditing requires by definition a global vision of the company. Also, the method of analysis adopted is qualitative and adapted to our study approach, but does not allow for generalization.

Several paths can be perceived to pursue this work. First of all, it is advisable to treat our theme by targeting other sectors of companies or other sizes in order to validate the procedure or to adapt it according to the case studied. It is therefore a question of testing the conclusions and proposals in samples of companies of different sizes and belonging to different activities. It is also possible to use IT tools to further develop this internal audit procedure of the cash cycle.

BIBLIOGRAPHIC REFERENCES

Abad, D., Sánchez-Ballesta, J. P., & Yagüe, J. (2017). Audit opinions and information asymmetry in the stock market. Accounting & finance, 57(2), 565-595.

Adams, M. B. (1994). Agency theory and the internal audit. Managerial auditing journal. 9(8), 8-12. https://doi.org/10.1108/02686909410071133

Alla, L., Hmioui, A., & Bentalha, B. (2020). La netnographie dans les recherches marketing: La communauté virtuelle comme consom'acteur vecteur d'efficacité marketing. Alternatives Managériales et Economiques, 4, 631-652.

Aschenbroich Y, Poloniato B., & Voyenne D., (1997), La Nouvelle trésorerie d'entreprise, 2e Edition, Dunod, Paris, 564 p.

Barbier E., (1995), L'audit interne : permanence et actualité, Editions d'organisation, P.21.

Becour J-C, Bouquin H. (2008), Audit operationnel (3e edition), Economica, 444 p.

Bentalha, B. (2020). Big-Data et Service Supply chain management: Challenges et opportunités. International Journal of Business and Technology Studies, 1(3).

Bentalha, B. (2022). Green Transportation Balanced Scorecard Model: A Fuzzy-Delphi Approach During COVID-19. In Computational Intelligence Techniques for Green Smart Cities (pp. 107-127). Springer, Cham.

Bentalha, B., & Hmioui, A. (2021). Smart Service Supply Chain and Just Walk Out Technology: A Netnographic Approach. In The Proceedings of the International Conference on Smart City Applications (pp. 223-236). Springer, Cham.

Bentalha, B., Hmioui, A., & Alla, L. (2019). The digitalization of the supply chain management of service companies: a prospective approach. In Proceedings of the 4th International Conference on Smart City Applications (pp. 1-8).

Bentalha, B., Hmioui, A., & Alla, L. (2020). The global performance of a service supply chain: a simulation-optimization under arena. In The Proceedings of the Third International Conference on Smart City Applications (pp. 489-502). Springer, Cham.

Bentalha, B., HMIOUI, A., & Alla, L. (2021). Last mile logistics applied to the distribution of COVID-19 vaccines: A prospection of good practices. Alternatives Managériales Economiques, 3(3), 41-61.

Bernard F., Gayraud R., Rousseau L. (2010), Contrôle interne, 3ème édition, Maxima, Paris, 327 pages.

Bernard F., Gayraud R., Rousseau L., (2008), Contrôle interne, 2ème édition, Edition Maxima, Paris, 299 pages.

Bragg, S. M. (2010). Treasury management: the Practitioner's Guide (Vol. 6). John Wiley & Sons.

Camerer, C. (1999). Behavioral economics: Reunifying psychology and economics. Proceedings of the National Academy of Sciences, 96(19), 10575-10577.

Carcary, M. (2020). The research audit trail: Methodological guidance for application in practice. Electronic Journal of Business Research Methods, 18(2), pp166-177.

Castanheira, N., Rodrigues, L. L., & Craig, R. (2010). Factors associated with the adoption of risk-based internal auditing. Managerial Auditing Journal.

Christopher, J.; Sarens, Gerrit; Leung, Philomena (2009). A critical analysis of the independence of the internal audit function: evidence from Australia, 22(2), 200–220.   doi:10.1108/09513570910933942

Chun, C. (1997). On the functions and objectives of internal audit and their underlying conditions. Managerial Auditing Journal.

De Zwaan, L., Stewart, J., & Subramaniam, N. (2011). Internal audit involvement in enterprise risk management. Managerial auditing journal.

Depallens G. & Jobard J.J. (1997), Gestion Financière de l'entreprise, 11ème Ed. Dunod, Paris.

El Menzhi K. (2011), la maîtrise des risques, indicateur majeur de performance du contrôle interne, Revue Marocaine de Recherche en Management et Marketing, N° 4-5.

Ernoult, T. (2012). Maquillage des comptes publics grecs : statistiques à la dérive ?. Regards croisés sur l'économie, 11, 113-115. https://doi.org/10.3917/rce.011.0113

Fatonah, S., Yulandari, A., & Wibowo, F. W. (2018). A review of e-payment system in e-commerce. In Journal of Physics: Conference Series, 1140(1). IOP Publishing.

Gervais M., (1983), Contrôle de gestion et planification de l'entreprise, Collection Gestion. Série Politique générale, finance et marketing, Economica, 512 p.

Gold, A., & Heilmann, M. (2019). The consequences of disclosing key audit matters (KAMs): A review of the academic literature. Maandblad voor accountancy en bedrijfseconomie, 93(1/2), 5-14.

Griffiths, P. (2016). Risk-based auditing. Routledge.

Helliar, C., & Dunne, T. (2004). Control of the treasury function. Corporate Governance: The international journal of business in society.

Hmioui, A., & Bentalha, B. (2020). Service Supply Chain Management et performance commerciale: Esquisse d'une synthèse théorique. Alternatives Managériales Economiques, 2(2), 1-21.

Hmioui, A., Alla L., & Bentalha, B. (2018). Proposition d'une démarche structurée de l'audit interne du cycle de trésorerie. Revue du contrôle, de la comptabilité et de l'audit, 2(2).

Hmioui, A., Alla, L., & Bentalha, B. (2021). Performance of ethical and conventional investment funds: comparison and contingencies. International Journal of Business Performance Management, 22(2-3), 219-235.

Hmioui, A., Bentalha, B., & Alla, L. (2020). Service supply chain: A prospective analysis of sustainable management for global performance. In 2020 IEEE 13th International Colloquium of Logistics and Supply Chain Management (LOGISTIQUA) (pp. 1-7). IEEE.

Hubert B., (1997), Trésorerie d'entreprise : gestion de liquidité et des risques, éditions DALLOZ, 680 p.

IAA-GLOBAL, (2013), Cadre de Référence International des pratiques professionnelles de l'audit interne, CRIPP, P 2 & 3.

IFACI (2006), Le management des risques de l'entreprise, éditions d'organisation, Paris, 338 p.

IFACI et Coopers & Lybrand, (1994), La nouvelle pratique du contrôle interne. Editions d'organisation, P 14.

IFACI et PriceWaterhouseCoopers, (2005), Le management des risques de l'entreprise : cadre de référence, techniques d'application, COSO II report. Editions d'Organisations, 2005, P 5, 9, 84, 123

IFACI, (2002), La pratique du contrôle interne, COSO Report, Editions d'Organisation, Collection Les Références, Paris.

IFACI, (2004), Les normes pour la pratique professionnelle de l'audit interne, Traduction et adaptation de : IIA, (2000, 2002), Standards for the Professional Practice of Internal Audit, Altamonte Springs, Florida: the Institute of Internal Auditors.

IFACI, (2011), Manuel d'Audit interne : Améliorer l'efficacité de la gouvernance, du contrôle interne et du management des risques., Traduction et adaptation de IIA – The Institute of Internal Auditor.

IFACI, (2012), Cadre de Référence International de l'Audit interne.

IFACI, PriceWaterhouseCoopers, Landwell, (2005), Le management des risques de l'entreprise : Cadre de référence – Techniques d'application, Editions d'Organisation, Collection Les Références, Paris.

IFACI. (2009). Enquête sur les pratiques de l'audit et du contrôle internes en France.

IIA, (2007), Internal Auditing : Assurance and Consulting Services, IIA Research Foundation, Altamonte Springs, Florida : the Institute of Internal Auditors.

Jensen M.C. et Meckling W.H., (1976), Theory of the firm: Managerial behavior, agency costs and ownership structure, Journal of Financial Economics, 3(4).

Jurakulovna, J. G., & Bahodirovich, R. U. (2021). Improving the Theoretical Framework of Internal Audit in the Corporate Governance System. Middle European Scientific Bulletin, 19, 345-348.

Koenig G. (1993), Production de la connaissance et constitution des pratiques organisationnelles, Revue de gestion des ressources humaines, n° 9, novembre, p.4-17.

Lamsiah, A., Benabderrazik, Y., & Bentalha, B. (2021). The Economic and political components of diplomatic discourse: State actors in Morocco-UK Free Trade Agreement as a case study. Alternatives Managériales Economiques, 3(4), 496-517.

Lee, S. H., Choi, S. U., & Ryu, J. Y. (2021). Do audit efforts increase the future equity value of client firm?. Managerial Auditing Journal.

Lemant O., (1995), La conduite d'une mission d'audit interne, méthodologie élaborée par un groupe de recherche de l'IFACI, DUNOD.

Manita et Chemangui, (2007), Les approches d'évaluation et les indicateurs de mesure de la qualité d'audit : une revue critique. Actes du 28ème Congrès de l'Association francophone de Comptabilité.

Matte P.H. (2002), un outil de gestion : la cartographie des risques à la régie des rentes du Québec, Revue française de l'audit interne, (n°167) : page 39.

Mautz, R.K., & Sharaf H.A., (1961), The Philosophy of Auditing, Sarasota, FL: American Accounting Association.

Meunier (2005), La trésorerie dans l'entreprise, Dunod, Paris

Mihret, D. G., James, K., & Mula, J. M. (2010). Antecedents and organisational performance implications of internal audit effectiveness: some propositions and research agenda. Pacific Accounting Review.

Mikol A., (1999), Les audits financiers, Editions d'Organisations, Paris,.

Mutchler, J. F. (2003). Independence and objectivity: a framework for research opportunities in internal auditing. Research opportunities in internal auditing, 231, 268.

Mutchler, J., Chang, S. and Prawitt, D. (2001), Independence and Objectivity: A Framework for Internal Auditors, The Institute of Internal Auditors Research Foundation, Altamonte Springs, FL

Newman, W., & Comfort, M. (2018). Investigating the value creation of internal audit and its impact on company performance. Academy of Entrepreneurship Journal, 24(3), 1-21.

Pérez-Cornejo, C., de Quevedo-Puente, E., & Delgado-García, J. B. (2019). How to manage corporate reputation? The effect of enterprise risk management systems and audit committees on corporate reputation. European Management Journal, 37(4), 505-515.

Phillot, M. (2021). US Treasury Auctions: A High Frequency Identification of Supply Shocks. Université de Lausanne, Faculté des hautes études commerciales (HEC), Département d'économie.

Pickett, S. (2000). Developing internal audit competencies. Managerial Auditing Journal.

Polak, P., Nelischer, C., Guo, H., & Robertson, D. C. (2020). "Intelligent" finance and treasury management: what we can expect. AI & SOCIETY, 35(3), 715-726.

Polak, P., Robertson, D. C., & Lind, M. (2011). The new role of the corporate treasurer: Emerging trends in response to the financial crisis. International Research Journal of Finance and Economics, (78).

Przybylska, J. M., & Kańduła, S. (2019). In Search of the Theory of Internal Audit. Torun Business Review, 18(3), 1-16.

Quinn, S., & Roberds, W. (2008). The evolution of the check as a means of payment: A historical survey. Economic Review, 93.

Rahman, M. M., Meah, M. R., & Chaudhory, N. U. (2019). The impact of audit characteristics on firm performance: an empirical study from an emerging economy. The Journal of Asian Finance, Economics and Business, 6(1), 59-69.

Renard J., (2006), Théorie et pratique de l'audit interne, Erolles, Editions d'organisation, P 91 & 92.

Renard. J., (2003), L'audit interne ce qui fait débat, Edition maxima, Paris.

Rousselot, P. & Verdié, J. (2017). Gestion de trésorerie. Dunod. 464 p.

Seol, I., Sarkis, J., & Lefley, F. (2011). Factor structure of the competency framework for internal auditing (CFIA) skills for entering level internal auditors. International Journal of Auditing, 15(3), 217-230.

Sinha, V. K., Engwall, M., & Strömsten, T. (2019). Cartography of Liquidity Risk Calculations.

Sion M. (2003), Gérer la trésorerie et la relation bancaire, Dunod, Paris, 271 P.

Śliwowski P., Wincewicz-Price A. (2019), Prościej, taniej i skuteczniej, czyli jak ekonomia behawioralna wspiera polityki publiczne w Polsce, Polski Instytut Ekonomiczny, Warszawa, http://pie.net.pl/wp-content/uploads/2019/06/ PIE-Raport_Behawio-ralna.pdf [access 11.08.2022].

Stewart, J. & Subramaniam, N. (2010). Internal audit independence and objectivity: emerging research opportunities. Managerial Auditing Journal, 25(4), 328–360. doi:10.1108/02686901011034162

Troi, S. M. (2018). The Importance of Audit and Internal Control Within an Organization. Scientific Bulletin-Economic Sciences, 17(3), 101-106.

Vatier R., (1989), Audit de la gestion sociale Edition d'organisation. 166 p.

Vernimmen P., Quiry, P.Y. Le Fur. (2009), Finance d'entreprise. Dalloz, Paris, 1200 p.

Von bertalanaffy L., (1991), Théorie générale des systèmes, Dunod, Paris.

Internal Audit of Treasury and cash management

TABLE OF CONTENTS

DEDICATION	vi
CONTENTS	vii
ACKNOWLEDGMENTS	viii
PREFACE	x
INTRODUCTION	1
PART ONE: THE THEORETICAL FRAMEWORK OF THE INTERNAL AUDIT OF THE CASH CYCLE	7
CHAPTER 1 : **THEORETICAL AND CONCEPTUAL APPROACHES TO INTERNAL AUDITING**	9
A) Definitions and evolution of internal auditing	10
B) Types of internal audit missions	15
C) The characteristics of internal auditing	16
D) Internal auditing standards	18
E) Competencies of the internal auditor	25
F) Internal audit as a risk management tool	26
G) Internal audit and related professions	30
a) internal and external auditing	30
b) Internal audit and management control	31
H) The internal audit approach	33
CHAPTER 2 : **THE COMPANY'S TREASURY**	34
A. Definition of cash flow (treasury)	34
B. The components of the treasury function	37
1. Liquidity management	37
2. Financial and liquidity risk management	37
C. The objectives of cash management	38
D. The company treasurer	39

Internal Audit of Treasury and cash management

E.	Current cash management challenges	41
1. Globalization		41
2. Expanding the role		41
3. Security		41
4. Regulation		41
CHAPTER 3 : **INTERNAL AUDIT OF THE TREASURY CYCLE**		42
A)	Objectives of the audit of treasury operations	42
B)	Delineation of auditable cash cycle transactions	43
a)	Payment control	43
1)	Payments by check or bank transfer	44
i.	Authorized signatures	44
ii.	Issuance of checks or money orders	44
iii.	Examination, verification, and cancellation of documents	45
2) Payment by cash		45
i.	Principle of cash payment	45
ii.	Signatures accepted in cash	46
iii.	Examination, Verification, and Cancellation of Documents	46
b) Control of receipts		46
i.	Cashing of checks	46
ii.	Cash Receipts	47
c) Financial costs of treasury operations		47
C) Retention of cash values		47
i.	Retention of checks	47
ii.	Check and Cash Deposit	47
iii.	Safeguarding of cash assets	48
D) Accounting of transactions in connection with the		48

treasury

i.	Segregation of duties	48
ii.	Monitoring of records	49
iii.	Bank Reconciliation	49

E) The internal audit approach of the treasury department 50

1) Overall completeness of accounting records 50

2) Examination of the control systems 50

3) Periodic monitoring of control systems 51

4) Specific examinations related to detour techniques 53

a) Possible embezzlement techniques 53

1) Embezzlement of revenues 53

2) Misappropriation of cash or bank balances 53

b) Special procedures and reviews 53

1) Bank reconciliation 53

2) Final consistency check 54

F) Internal audit tools for the cash cycle 54

1. Information gathering instruments 54
- The audit interview 54
- Direct observation 54
- The questionnaire 55
- Statistical surveys 55

2. Descriptive methods 55
- Flowcharts 55
- The narrative 56
- The diagrams 56
- Separation of duties grids 57
- The Problem Analysis and Revelation Sheet 57

3. The tools of knowledge and diagnosis 57

4. Validation techniques 58

o	Arithmetic and valuation checks	58
o	Document control	58
o	Third Party Confirmation	58
o	Computerized tools	58

Part Two: **Internal Audit of the Treasury Cycle: Practical Aspects** — 60

CHAPTER 1: **METHODOLOGY, OBJECTIVES AND DETAILED APPROACH OF THE CASH CYCLE AUDIT** — 61

A)	Preliminary audit phase	65
B)	Detailed audit phase	65
C)	Synthesis and completion phase	65

CHAPTER 2: **A PRACTICAL APPROACH TO THE INTERNAL AUDIT OF THE CASH CYCLE** — 66

A/ The preliminary phase of the audit — 66

A-1) Knowledge of the entity and its environment — 67

A-2) Description of the tasks — 72

A-3) Diagnosis of procedures — 73

1)	Payment of national suppliers	74
2)	Payment of international suppliers	77
3)	Cash payment	78

A-4) Risk analysis and risk register — 78

A-5) Significance thresholds — 91

A-6) The overall internal audit strategy — 93

B) Detailed audit of the cash cycle — 96

B-1) Segregation of duties grid: — 96

B-2) The internal control questionnaire — 99

B-3) The detailed plan of the cash flow audit — 104

B-4) Treasury control: Compliance tests on the — 113

expenditure system

B-5) Continuity testing on the preparation and verification of bank reconciliation statements	118
B-6) Document Control	120
B-7) Third-party confirmation	122
B-8) The Payment Dashboard	124
B-9) Treasury reporting	128
B-10) Bank commission tracking form	130
B-11) Currency conversion form	132
B-12) Discount follow-up	134
C/ The audit summary phase	136
CHAPTER 3: **RECOMMENDATIONS AND PERSPECTIVES OF THE INTERNAL AUDIT OF THE TREASURY CYCLE**	144
CONCLUSION	150
BIBLIOGRAPHIC REFERENCES	153
TABLE OF CONTENTS	158
ABOUT THE AUTHOR	163

ABOUT THE AUTHOR

Badr Bentalha received his Ph.D. in Service Logistics and performance at Sidi Mohammed Ben Abdellah University, Fez, Morocco. He is an Associate Professor in Economics and Management. He has written several articles and participated in various international conferences. He is a member of numerous scientific committees of international journals and conferences. Since 2009, Mr. Bentalha has helped sundry companies implement an audit system, resolve issues and improve performance.

www.ingramcontent.com/pod-product-compliance
Lightning Source LLC
Chambersburg PA
CBHW052353220526
45465CB00003BA/1092